Synopsis of American Elementary Education: The Longest Pandemic

American Elementary Education: The Longest Pandemic examines the current state of American elementary education. Although there are some excellent charter and public schools, the general performance of most students, particularly in kindergarten through sixth grade, is poor as compared to many other international programs. This book discusses the problems that abound in many elementary schools and provides solutions to help address the conditions that result in poor student performance. The information in *The Longest Pandemic* is supported by effective school research, thus providing information that helps to address the deficiencies of American elementary education. It provides strategies to help parents, teachers, and school board members understand problems and help them evaluate their own school programs. The book presents historical information with an actual case study noting the beginning of the slide to mediocrity in a school that once was one of the most successful elementary programs in Arizona and the country. The information provided in *The Longest Pandemic* will help readers deal with educational issues, not only in instruction, but also with the influence of teacher unions and controversies such as the critical race theory. The author of this book is a former teacher, principal, superintendent, and college adjunct professor. He uses his own experience to illustrate the

i

politics that influence the quality of elementary instruction. *The Longest Pandemic* provides readers with a concrete tool to help fully understand the problems in American elementary education.

AMERICAN ELEMENTARY EDUCATION:

THE LONGEST PANDEMIC

AMERICAN ELEMENTARY EDUCATION:

THE LONGEST PANDEMIC

The Problem with American Elementary Education and What Parents Can Do About It

Dr. Patrick M. Dallabetta

Xulon Press

Xulon Press
2301 Lucien Way #415
Maitland, FL 32751
407.339.4217
www.xulonpress.com

Paperback ISBN-13: 978-1-66286-494-0
Ebook ISBN-13: 978-1-66286-495-7

DEDICATION

This book is dedicated to my wife Pamela Kay. She has been a great partner and an excellent role model for our two girls. Tamara Leigh and Kimberley Anne have been very successful in education. I was their administrator during their entire public school education, something I felt was a great benefit, although, I am not so sure they felt the same. They have made me proud by raising six wonderful grandchildren who have also achieved at high levels and readily accepted the importance of education. I would especially like to thank my former superintendent and the governing board of the fundamental school district described in this book. They cared deeply about children and generously offered their encouragement and support during the development of the fundamental school I will describe in *The Longest Pandemic*. They had enough faith in the school to stand in line to enroll their own children in a program they knew would be tremendously successful. I would like to recognize the thousands of public school students and the college students I served for more than 37 years. Lastly, I am grateful to my post-graduate students, especially those who chose public school teaching and administration as a career. I am hoping they accept the responsibility to use effective school methods and research, again making American elementary education the best in the world.

TABLE OF CONTENTS

INTRODUCTION

Except for the millions of people who lost their lives during the coronavirus pandemic, the generally poor quality of public elementary education is, in many ways, a much longer and serious pandemic. The virus has made life miserable for our children and literally destroyed many lives. The pandemic dealt education a serious blow and it will take a long time to make up for lost instruction.

Unfortunately, the general quality of many of our public elementary schools has been consistently poor for many years and, with the public health crisis, made it even worse for most of our elementary school children. They have suffered emotionally and have certainly lost even more academically. Teachers and administrators are worried that spring testing assessments will show how much learning has been lost in the past two years. The fact is the general quality of elementary education has been suffering for many years. What will it take for American parents to understand the impact of this almost century-long pandemic?

American Elementary Education: The Longest Pandemic will examine the current state of elementary education in America so that readers will understand why so many school children are not performing adequately. This book will help parents better understand the importance of a strong elementary school foundation of skills for their children. Parents will learn what makes a school successful and will help them evaluate options to ensure their children are enrolled in the best possible elementary school programs.

Without a solid foundation of skills, many children will struggle for their entire lives. The quality of instruction children receive, especially in early elementary school, may be a forecast of how successful they will be in middle and high school.

Marva Collins, the founder of the Westside Preparatory School in Chicago, Illinois, formerly one of the nation's most successful private elementary school programs, shared the following with her primary students in one of their first days in school.

"I know most of you can't spell your name. You don't know the alphabet, you don't know how to read, you don't know homonyms or how to syllabicate. I promise you that you will. None of you has ever failed. School may have failed you. Well goodbye to failure, children. Welcome to success. You will read hard books in here and understand what you read. You will write everyday so that writing becomes second nature to you. You will memorize a poem every week so that you can train your minds to remember things. It is useless for you to learn something in school if you are not going to remember it."[1]

Collin's students were entirely inner-city minority African-American students who were failing in Chicago Public Schools. Yet she helped them achieve at incredible levels.[2]

Our children continue to fail at an alarming rate. What can you do as parents to enroll your children in the best schools? What is a quality instructional program? What makes a good school?

I will help you understand what quality is all about and help you make sure your children have a better chance to succeed. I will discuss educational alternatives and give you strategies to ensure you will know what teachers and schools must do to succeed.

I have avoided referencing many specific schools and districts. The decision not to identify specific school programs was difficult. Naming specific schools or districts will not change the purpose of this book as it is the situation that is most important, something that can happen anywhere in the country.

Much of the information I offer is based on my experiences in Arizona and districts in the west. Arizona is no different than any other state in the nation. I have had many other direct experiences in several states, including Colorado and Oregon, so the information in this book is typical of other schools and districts all over the United States.

It is important to note that not all schools and districts are bad. There are many excellent school programs, some beyond what many think possible in today's educational environment. Unfortunately, I have seen far too many very poor programs. Those experiences convinced me that it would be helpful to tell it like it is, both good and bad.

Most of the people I spoke to regarding *The Longest Pandemic* seem dedicated to helping and are trying to develop good programs. Unfortunately, many of the most dedicated educators don't seem to understand what is required to create the most effective instructional programs. I am especially grateful to those people who were honest in discussing their respective programs, while providing information that gives me hope for the future of education.

At one time in my career, I was the President of the Superintendents Division of Arizona School Administrators during the legislative effort to allow school vouchers and provide Arizona public funds for charter schools. During that time, most of my colleagues were more concerned with the possible approval of a school voucher program than the charter school approval effort. I was unsuccessful in convincing them that charter school programs would ultimately attract many more students than a pilot voucher school program. I anticipated the loss of many public school students because charter schools have more program flexibility.

It is much easier to impose new standards and build a quality program and staff than attempting to change the program in an existing school.

After the Arizona Legislature approved charters and early in the charter school movement, I served as the hearing officer to consider the possible revocation of one of the first charter school programs in the state. That charter school was fraught with corruption and after the total situation was presented, I recommended the charter be revoked. However, I knew it was inevitable that competent and knowledgeable charter school educators would be given an opportunity to change education forever.

Many successful charter school programs have evolved into viable alternatives for parents and their children. Unfortunately, the general quality of public elementary schools in America continues to decline. Articles in many Arizona newspapers described how education in that state was the third worst in the United States. The fact that Arizona elementary schools are rated so low really hits home to me since I spent most of my experience in the state. Something has to be done and our parents can effectuate change quickly and effectively with the right information.

Few politicians seem concerned about the quality of American education other than making the effort to improve teacher compensation programs and attract more competent teachers. However, in history there were two significant exceptions. President Ronald Reagan established the National Commission on Excellence in Education that produced the report *A Nation of Risk: The Imperative for Educational Reform.*[3] Secondly, President George Bush established the legislation for the No Child Left Behind (NCLB) effort.[4] The NCLB program required states to annually test students in reading and math in grades 3-8. Since those efforts, it seems little has been done nationally to improve or raise educational standards.

I continue to be concerned for the performance of the elementary schools as a former teacher, principal, school superintendent, college professor, and now grandfather.

The Longest Pandemic will focus primarily on elementary education. However, many of the concepts shared in this book can be applied to all school levels. This book is designed to educate parents and help them understand there are many school options available. In the past 25 years, those options have increased to include public charter schools. Regardless, parents need to learn more about the academic effectiveness of their children's school. This book will also assist parents to establish a plan of action and be more proactive in dealing with poor or ineffective elementary school education.

Choosing the best school for children is not difficult if parents apply the information and tools provided in *The Longest Pandemic*. Reading this book will provide some simple strategies to help kick-start parents to get more involved. *The Longest Pandemic* includes a questionnaire parents can use to interview a teacher or principal. The answers to the interview questions will provide parents with program information that should help them understand the quality of a school program. The questionnaire will also give parents the information they need to help provide instructional support for their children.

I encourage parents to read the supporting information in this book. Doing so will help better clarify the foundation for the tools I am offering. I hope you enjoy *The Longest Pandemic!*

Chapter 1

PERFORMANCE INFORMATION

The publication Education Week ranked all our states according to student performance.[5] It used student performance as the most important component of their ranking system. The rankings were also based on a K-12 system, somewhat beyond our emphasis on K-6 elementary education. However, using letter grades is a simple way to rate education in our nation. In short, our country was given a national grade of C in performance. The sad fact is that not one state in the nation received a letter grade of A, although Massachusetts was assigned a B+. New Jersey, and Virginia were the only states receiving a B grade. The majority of our states received a C grade. The following states received some form of an even worse grade:

Kansas (D+)
Delaware (D+)
South Dakota (D+)
Missouri (D+)
Montana (D+)
Michigan (D+)

North Dakota (D+)
Nevada (D+)
North Dakota (D+)
West Virginia (D+)
District of Columbia (D)
Alabama (D)
Oregon (D)
Arkansas (D)
Mississippi (D)
Oklahoma (D)
South Carolina (D)
Alaska (D)
New Mexico (D)
Louisiana (D)

The fact that only a few states received a decent grade report is simply crazy!

How does education in the United States compare to other nations?

If you believe one of the keys to our country's success is education, the United States is losing big time! The quality of our educational system has faltered and we are falling further and further behind many countries, some of which are considered "third world." The debate goes on as to what is wrong and what can be done to stop the bleeding. The answer isn't rocket science and it doesn't take a genius to figure out what is wrong and what can be done to help resolve the issue. Although I believe everyone wants better education in the United States, you can't fix something you don't understand. I believe many of the most important stakeholders don't understand what can be done to deal with current educational problems. Further, too many educators are not willing to rock the boat!

U.S. students continue to rank around the middle of the pack and behind many other industrial nations. As a lifetime educator, I see this situation as depressing. The Program for International Student Assessment (PISA) is given every third year and measures reading ability, math, and science literacy, and other key skills of 15-year-old students in dozens of developed and developing countries.[6] Students' skills are formed in elementary education. A recent PISA test in 2018 placed U.S. students just above average in reading and science but below average in mathematics.

Perhaps one of the more common international tests, the (NAEP) National Assessment of Educational Progress,[7] also referred to as the "Nation's Report Card," is a project of the U.S. Department of Education. The assessment provides important data for Americans. The average 2015 NAEP math scores for fourth and eighth-grade students fell for the first time since 1990. 29 percent of American eighth-graders fell below levels considered basic while 18 percent of fourth graders performed below basic levels. Sadly, students from such countries as Macao, Estonia, Latvia, and Slovenia outperformed American students. The 2015 NAEP rated 40 percent of fourth graders, 33 percent of eighth graders, and 25 percent of 12th graders as "proficient" or "advanced" in math. Despite the efforts of some researchers to show that American public schools are doing well, the assessments support the fact that improvement is needed. It will get worse with future testing efforts, especially considering the pandemic.

U.S. students' academic achievement lags behind that of their peers in many other countries. Although U.S. students were making progress in mathematics, the latest scores of both fourth, and eighth-grade students worsened, according to the international tests in Trends in International Mathematics and Science Study.[8] The results of the NAEP assessment indicated 12th-grade students are, at best, average. In 2015, 38 percent of fourth-graders, 34 percent of eighth-graders, and 22 percent of 12th-graders were rated proficient or better in science; 24 percent of fourth-graders, 32 percent of eighth-graders and 40 percent of twelfth-graders were rated "below basic." Internationally, the U.S. stands in the middle of the pack in science, math, and reading scores.[9]

The Progress in International Reading Literacy Study compared the reading ability of a large number of participating countries.[10] Unfortunately the United States ranked lower than 15 countries in fourth-grade reading literacy. U.S. students had lower scores than the previous testing cycle. A sobering fact is the Russian Federation topped all the countries tested and outscored the students in the United States by a significant 63 scale points.

The United States now ranks near the bottom of 35 industrialized nations in mathematics.[11] Family financial status seems to have an influence on student performance. The distance in test scores between the highest performing and the lowest performing nations is much greater, even though educational programs in the United States tend to focus on lower performing students. Although the debate about student performance continues, all factors indicate the need for educational reform in our country. According to Arne Duncan, Secretary of Education serving President Barack Obama, "The hard truth is that the U.S. is not among the top-performing OECD in any subject tested by PISA."[12] Ironically, few politicians seem concerned, based on the lack of current action to try, and help improve American education.

My question is, are we to be satisfied with average student performance at best?

Chapter 2

UNDERSTANDING THE PROBLEM

The decline in the quality of American elementary education is certainly among the most serious pandemics in our country. According to *The American Heritage Dictionary*, a pandemic is something that occurs over a wide geographic area and affects an exceptionally high proportion of the population.[13] After 37 years in education, I am most concerned about the overall quality of our elementary schools and, in many cases, it's a situation so bad that it constitutes nothing less than an educational pandemic. American students need a solid foundation of skills in elementary school. When that foundation is weak, students will struggle later in school and perhaps even in their lives!

Parents should be concerned with both how and what students are taught as there are many problems to be addressed in American elementary education. They include many instances of poor elementary instructional curriculum and methods. The inclusion of critical race theory in some schools provides us with just one example of what can happen in our schools without parents' knowledge and it will create even worse outcomes.

Fortunately, our parents have begun to focus on what is taught in our schools because of the critical race theory topic. There are many other problems in elementary education that parents do not understand, and I hope to bring those problems to light. If you believe one of our country's educational successes is a solid foundation of academic skills in most elementary schools, you are wrong. Too many educators either can't or won't do anything to change the system. Although I believe Americans want better elementary education in the United States, you can't fix something you don't understand.

While there are many very good charter, parochial, and public schools in America, there are far too many public elementary schools that are simply not effective, and the situation is getting worse. The concerns and the problems to be discussed in *The Longest Pandemic* are by no means new, such as the quality of elementary reading instruction that was a source of discourse for many years, perhaps beginning with Rudolph Flesch who published *Why Johnny Can't Read* in 1955.[14] His paperback, also a feature in *Reader's Digest*, became one of the most famous publications at the time to deal with the state of elementary school teaching methods. Flesch wrote the book because of his interactions as a tutor of a 12-year-old student "Johnny" who was retained in sixth grade because he could not read and was likely unable to be successful in middle school. After extensive observations and research into elementary school instruction, he concluded, "The teaching of reading all over the United States, in all the schools, in all the textbooks is totally wrong and flies in the face of all logic and common sense." While Flesch wrote the book as a generalized opinion, the basics of what he believed should help us understand some of the current problems, particularly in primary grade reading instruction. The problems he eluded to still exist.

Mary Burkhardt, the former director of the Department of Reading in the Rochester New York City School District, wrote the Foreword in Flesch's second book *Why Johnny Still Can't Read*.[15] She describes her frustration as a primary school student learning to read which made her own early elementary years a bad experience. She was taught using a "look-say" method of instruction. Eventually her grandmother taught her to use phonics and the sounds of letters and combinations of letters. Her own early failures as a beginning reader helped her appreciate the lack of reading skills of her junior and senior high school students in her first teaching position. Those initial experiences as a teacher inspired her to become a remedial reading teacher in an elementary school.

As a result of her teaching successes, Burkhardt eventually became the district's director of reading, influencing the district to move to a phonics-based reading program. She believed children with reading difficulties were the victims of poor primary reading instruction. I agree with her observation.

"Obviously, the lesson for us is that children come to school with a tremendously rich listening and speaking vocabulary. As soon as they are able to sound out words, they can enter them into their reading and spelling vocabulary. Once they can decode a word, then they may automatically know the meaning. If the word that's read is totally new to the child, he can then immediately be taught its meaning."[16]

Besides a myriad of information regarding the quality of American Education, not much has been done since the early 1980's. President Ronald Reagan did bring the discussions to the forefront by establishing The National Commission on Excellence in Education, an independent commission that published *A Nation at Risk*.[17] The commission recommended what can be done to improve education. The purpose of the commission was to examine the quality of education in our country and to report to the President and Nation the practical recommendations for improvement.

Sadly, some educators referred to the *A Nation at Risk* as "crisis rhetoric" and there are likely few contemporary educators that are seemingly even aware of the report. The National Commission on Excellence in Education made several important summary recommendations. These recommendations included the following:

1. **Improve leadership and management in the schools**. Better training for administrators is necessary, and they should be paid according to their performance.

2. **Devote significantly more time to learning**. This included more homework, early grade instruction in study and work skills, improve attendance, and reduce administrative burdens.

3. **Express a new and higher regard for teachers**. This included better recruitment, raising standards, providing financial assistance to attract better teachers, improving educational certification, improving pay commensurate with performance, improving professional development, and tightening procedures for teacher dismissal.

4. **Spend education dollars more effectively**.

5. **Create business/education partnerships**.

6. **Create partnerships between various educational institutions**.

7. **Make the academic experience more intense and productive**. This includes discipline, attendance, homework, and grades.

8. **Use rigorous and challenging course work**.

9. **Promote students based on ability, not age**.

10. **Identify the level and ability of students at major transition points**.

11. **Better address the needs of underserved students**.[18]

Addressing the Recommendations of A *Nation at Risk*

Recommendation 1: Improve leadership and management in the schools. I enjoyed my university teacher education program at a college, originally founded as a teacher's college. I learned a lot, respected my professors, and eventually gained certification as an elementary and secondary teacher, elementary and secondary principal, and superintendent. I finished a doctorate in education with an emphasis on public school administration.

My doctoral program instruction was mostly philosophical in nature. I became close friends with many of my professors and believe they made every effort to prepare me for my career in education. However, my education at the doctoral level in educational administration was not very practical. While a firm philosophical basis may be needed, I felt as if I had been "thrown to the wolves" in my first administrative position and was seriously lacking in the knowledge of practical issues to which I was to respond as a new principal.

While I initially may or may not have been effective as an administrator, I was a quick learner. Later in my career in my first district office position, my superintendent and I began to look at other programs that were successful in producing higher levels of student performance to help instruction become more effective. We looked at successful programs and reviewed a huge amount of research in various subjects from effective instruction to positive classroom management. We visited as many outstanding programs as possible. My superintendent and I were competitive by nature and we wanted our programs to be the best. We analyzed in detail the most effective instructional programs. We looked at the factors that resulted in both good and bad programs.

The frustrating thing about my own efforts was learning that many of our current problems result from poor school administration. While educational excellence begins with the district's governing board and superintendent, the principal is perhaps the most important person in any public-school program. I found that many of the problems in elementary education resulted from poor local school management in combination with a lack of district-level support.

Governing board members are generally not professional educators and they should not be expected to grasp the reasons why schools are good or bad. They often fail to examine the performance of students in their schools. They should insist that schools provide annual academic achievement information and expect school administrators to develop strategies for improving student performance.

Recommendation 2: Devote significantly more time to learning. Many administrators barely touch on the issue of instructional time and the length of the school day. The instructional time we have to teach is sacred and should be utilized effectively. The commission recommended that additional training is needed if more time should be added to the instructional calendar. I find this especially interesting since I dealt with the issue of the amount of time we teach extensively in the presentation

Maximizing Learning Time: Practical Strategies from Experience and Research,[19] a presentation to the National Academy of School Executives. I focused on effective research as a foundation to assist in developing the programs that were proven to be hugely successful.

Clearly the following is most important:

1. The amount of time teachers allocate to instruction in a particular curriculum content area is positively associated with student learning in that content area.

2. The proportion of allocated time that students are engaged is positively associated with learning.

3. The proportion of time that reading or mathematics tasks are performed with success is positively associated with student learning. The proportion of time that reading or mathematics tasks are performed with low success is negatively associated with student learning.

4. Increases in academic learning time are not associated with more negative attitudes toward mathematics, reading, or school.[20]

Now is there anybody who believes our students have not lost even more in the last years of chaos during the pandemic?

Research on classroom priorities and time spent on various subject areas is critical if schools are to be effective. Classroom environment and student management are also important in creating excellence. Researchers have proven that student's achievement is higher when students spend more time engaged in learning activities. Not the least bit surprising is the fact that the amount of time students spend learning in the important basic subjects differs dramatically from classroom to classroom and school to school.[21]

Chapter 3

FUNDAMENTAL SCHOOL MAGNET PROGRAM: WHAT CAN GO WRONG

After the publication of *A Nation At Risk*, the governing board and administration of the district where I worked implemented many changes. One of those changes was to develop a fundamental elementary school magnet program to serve as a model for other schools. Please note that the terms fundamental, basic, and traditional are interchangeable in *The Longest Pandemic*.

It would be difficult to fully understand why I am writing this book without knowing how I came to worry about the effectiveness of elementary education in America. The more I became involved in elementary education the more I felt American elementary education was "missing the boat." I had only one opportunity to physically build a new school and install a completely new instructional program. I was serious about making it the best possible school. I was encouraged to do whatever I felt necessary to create a model of school excellence. I carefully reviewed effective school research and visited some of the best-performing elementary schools in the state and nation. This opportunity was afforded to me by a wonderfully supportive school board and superintendent who had complete faith in my ability to build a model curriculum, different from most elementary schools in the district, county, state, and even the nation. I seized upon the opportunity because I knew we could improve elementary instruction and build a program that could be a model for elementary schools. Much of what was created is supported by educational research, and in many cases, even used in some charter, parochial, and public schools.

This is what happened!

A newly elected school board hired a new superintendent to replace a long-tenured superintendent. Their reasoning for this action was founded on poor student achievement and perceived poor behavior in the district. The new school board was clear in its direction to deal with these issues and believed they were elected to make positive changes. They were not afraid to impose new and higher expectations.

The former superintendent was popular in the community even though the general student performance of students was poor as compared to other schools and districts in the area. The former superintendent was likable, and his teachers and employees were, for the most part, supportive of their district's leader.

The change in the governing board resulted in some discontent in the community and district. How could the new school board treat the former superintendent, a fine man who, while still employed, had a school named in his honor? Regardless, the school board terminated the superintendent and hired someone new, who was charged with the responsibility to improve student performance and change the reputation of the district.

The new superintendent was a risk-taker and knew that he would need to make many difficult but important changes. The changes he made resulted in some uneasiness among the staff. He was not afraid of controversy and did his best to support the direction of the new school board. He was also very competitive and wanted to make the district the best among the other five districts in the area.

While many patrons in the district supported the effort to change, there remained a sizable amount of discontent among many of the former superintendent's friends, including some of the teaching staff. The new superintendent began to build a new team and replaced some district office staff. I was hired perhaps because I was the former principal of one of the highest performing elementary schools in the state. I had grown up in the community and had extensive experience in special education, federal projects, curriculum, and instruction. Thus began an educational friendship and partnership that helped create an elementary school and district that gained both state and national recognition.

The administration moved to exert more control of the instructional program. At that time, there were no consistent curriculum standards, and in many cases the choice of instruction, materials, and methods was completely up to individual teachers and whatever instructional program they were using. The district developed a new curriculum guide for reading, language arts, and mathematics in an effort to organize and prioritize instruction. The task was enormous and the teachers were generally supportive of the effort, perhaps due to a lack of instructional direction in the past. The new curriculum guide was built on the instructional skills most basic and important to each grade level.

None of the important skills at each grade level were ever challenged by any of the principals or teaching staff. It is interesting to note the new curriculum guide included instructional objectives that were normally included in subsequent grade levels, thus attempting to accelerate the skills to be taught. As an example, the new first-grade curriculum included some skills normally taught at the second-grade level. Surprisingly, none of the teachers questioned the accelerated skills, and I believe they welcomed the efforts for more consistency overall.

New instructional materials were purchased and most importantly, the district developed recommendations for how much time should be devoted to the most important subjects of reading, language arts, and mathematics.

Our efforts to align the curriculum with the state-mandated testing program remain a source of some discourse among educators. It is important to note that we did not teach the test but did make sure our instructional program included the skills tested in the state's mandated testing program. We recognized the importance of focusing on the most important skills required for mastery at each grade level.

Notice that the term "core" was not utilized, bringing into focus yet another subject of some controversy. After the community's schools test results were published in the local newspaper, an anonymous source accused the district of actually "teaching the test" because of the incredible improvement in student performance. That accusation was later dismissed after an investigation by the State Department of Education.

More History

At that time, the district owned a new school site and had enough unused bond money from a previous bond issue to build a new elementary school. This was important due to increasing enrollment and the fact that the district had some of the best land in the community available for new home construction. The district encompassed a significant agricultural area and was composed of a large number of limited English and non-English speaking children.

The existing schools in the district were already physically located so close to each other that the administration recommended the governing board build a new elementary school without having to redistrict student attendance zones. This presented the district with a huge potential problem because any district that requires a redistricting of school attendance zones will likely exacerbate the potential for parent dissatisfaction. However, the situation presented a perfect opportunity to offer an alternative program that would be made available to all students in the district.

A proposal was made to develop a "magnet" program to avoid redistricting. In education, the term "magnet" was formerly used in an effort to desegregate schools.

This was not the case with our effort. We simply wanted to build a program that would excite parents and attract students from the entire district without having to create new school attendance zones. We also wanted to eliminate the need to purchase more buses and create new bus routes.

At that time, the amount of bond money available to the district limited the funding for the capital purchase of more buses and kitchen equipment. The district did include some of the infrastructure for future busing and kitchen service programs in the construction project. We anticipated the school might someday want to provide a lunch service program. In the interim, the district's new magnet program would require parents to provide transportation and lunches for their students.

The new school board was very enthusiastic and supportive of the entire project. However, the question remained, what kind of alternative program would entice parents to provide transportation and food service for their children at the new school?

The governing board proceeded with the construction of a new school with the provision that the district would create a "magnet" program to incorporate all factors we felt would be a model for instructional effectiveness at other schools. The governing board approved the recommendation and the superintendent asked me to work with interested parents to help create a philosophical foundation for the new elementary school magnet program.

A pilot program was developed and implemented while the new school was being built and tested with six grades (first through sixth grade) located in portable buildings at one of the existing schools. Parents agreed to provide transportation and lunches for their children if they wanted to participate in the magnet pilot program. Work with the parents proceeded in the spring semester and early summer. The administration agreed to create a "basic, fundamental, or traditional" elementary program that we hoped would support the effort to improve the curricular program of the entire school district.

During our research and attempts to visit high-performing schools, we became very interested in successful programs both in the state and nation. We were most impressed with the Benjamin Franklin Basic School in Mesa, Arizona. That school was also a basic magnet school whose student scores on the state test were among the best in Arizona. Parent interest in that school was tremendous, and so much so that they routinely camped out prior to registration to get their children enrolled in the school.

We also became interested in other schools in the country that were proven successful in producing high student achievement. Although now no longer in existence, I was particularly impressed with Marva Collin's Westside Preparatory School in Chicago, Illinois. I was fortunate to have met and talked extensively with her as a presenter at a Reading Reform Conference in Washington, D.C. Collins built one of the most successful private schools in America. My personal interactions with her were among the most important in my life. For interested parents I suggest reading *Marva Collins' Way*.[22]

We convinced the parents to support the design of the curriculum for the new school to meet the existing bond funding constraints, with the provision that it cover all the more basic skills and implement a more "traditional or fundamental" school program. An entire year was spent on the physical construction and the instructional program. The parents were excited and overwhelmingly supported the fundamental school proposal. Numerous meetings were held, with both English-speaking and non-English speaking parents, to help develop a pilot program while the new school was being built. Eventually the term "fundamental" was even included in the name of the school.

As mentioned, the construction project included some of the kitchen infrastructure for a future lunch program. When most of a school's population consists of children who qualify for free lunches, the entire school qualifies for federal subsidies to help support a free lunch program. However, the parents agreed to provide "brown bag" lunches for their children. In addition, the parents would provide transportation for their children, thus making it a true magnet program.

Surprisingly, the fact that parents would need to provide student lunches and provide their own transportation to school never created any major issue. Everyone lived close enough to the school and, in some cases, parents even created transportation pools to get the children to school. The initial money saved by not providing lunch and transportation programs, helped the district provide a before-and-after school resource program at the new school.

The school resource program included a computer lab (I am proud to note one of the first networked elementary school computer labs in the nation), science lab, tutoring assistance, English and Spanish tutoring, and sports program. Parents who wanted their children to participate in the resource program could drop off children as early as 7:30 a.m. and pick them up as late as 4:30 p.m. We were told parents, especially working parents, were anxious to enroll their children in the school. The optional hours of school operation provided most children and parents with an extended school day. The teachers were paid extra stipends to participate in the resource program.

The first of the computer labs was built at one of the other elementary schools and tested during construction of the new school. The computer equipment was not used for fun and games but to augment the instructional program. I believe the administration was aware of the potentially positive impact of technology on education, well before it became a staple in most schools.

Other Curriculum Changes for the New Fundamental School

Science instruction was to emphasize the use of the scientific method. Appropriate grade level instructional activities were developed and science experiments required the students to utilize the scientific method in a school lab situation.

Ask a Question.... Complete Background Research.... Develop a Hypothesis.... Test the Hypothesis with an Experiment.... Evaluate Results by Analyzing Data.... Examine the Original Hypothesis.... Communicate the Results of the Experiment

The physical education program was built on the President's Physical Fitness Challenge goals, and first introduced during the Lyndon Johnson presidency. The President's Physical Fitness Challenge is an American program promulgated by the President's Council on Physical Fitness.[23] The program encourages students to engage in sports and nutrition that aimed to "make being active part of their everyday lives and to be physically fit."

Approximately 80 percent of the students earned presidential recognition by the end of the first year of the pilot program. The students were required to participate in physically appropriate tests, using such things as curl-ups, shuttle runs, endurance runs or walks, pull-ups, flexed-arm hangs, and sit-ups. I recall the frustration of my youngest daughter, who was worried that she might not be able to do even one pull-up (a requirement at her age). But she was able to meet that requirement before the final tests were administered.

At that time, I was a runner and ran regularly with many of the students in the program. After the first year of the program, approximately a third of the students at the school were regularly running long distances. A team of seven students even completed a relay run from Tecate to Ensenada, Mexico, a long-distance relay run of 85 miles crossing the Sierra Madre Mountains. The students ran with adult runners. The team was made up of students as young as seven years old and the Nike Company donated complete uniforms for the entire elementary school team. The school later sponsored a 10k race to help raise money for the renovation of the Statue of Liberty, an activity that supported the school's emphasis on patriotism. All the school's activities gained favorable media coverage.

The social studies program emphasized American history and built on the importance of patriotism. The students later even picked *Patriots* as their school mascot name. It is my opinion that the eventual name of the school and choice of mascots, not to mention the hopes of encouraging patriotism, irritated some more liberal parents and teachers in the community.

During the pilot program I met with my college advisor and close friend who bluntly said he was disappointed in me even though he had considered me his best ever graduate student. That really hurt me, and I asked him what was the problem? He was most upset with the school's name, which was chosen by the students and named to honor the Republican president at the time. He was also upset that we had built a "fundamental" school. He told me "All schools teach the fundamental skills." I tried to explain what we were doing and asked him to wait and see how the children performed.

I never heard from him again after the students' performance received statewide recognition for outstanding achievement. Sadly, we never spoke again, and he passed just a few years later. I'm sure he learned about the superior performance of the students, but I never had the chance to talk to him about what had been accomplished. That one incident led me to the belief that many college professors lean far too much to the left. They seem to try and indoctrinate students into more liberal philosophies. Whatever happened to giving students facts and then allowing them to develop their own philosophies?

Regardless, each classroom in the fundamental school was required to present a short patriotic program (and it often included memorization) at a flag-raising ceremony each week after which the entire student body recited the Pledge of Allegiance. Rote memory requirements were an important part of the entire program. Long ago many educators believed in a philosophy that "the mind is a muscle and must be exercised to remain healthy." Unfortunately, patriotism and the love of our nation have been slowly eradicated from American school programs. The flag-raising ceremony on the first day of the fundamental school, where the entire school student body assembled, created quite a stir in the community, prompting calls from neighbors close to the school to find out "what is wrong at the school," and "was there an emergency?" I still find that incredible to this day.

Another missing element in contemporary social studies programs is geography. It is a subject dear to my heart since I studied geography in both my bachelor and master's degree programs. Sadly, it is my belief that most American students are geographically illiterate. Social studies programs should include both the physical and cultural aspects of a geography program. If you don't believe me, just ask any young student to locate Crimea on a map and explain why it may be important to Russia. Try asking any upper-grade student to name the major continents or why are the Suez and Panama Canals are important to the world economy. Although I left the district the year the new school opened, my original plan to include the subject of geography as an integral part of the social studies program may never have materialized.

Most importantly, the fundamental school program included a phonics-based reading and writing program that I will describe in more detail later.

We bought used mathematics books authored by a Christian book company because those books included lots of math problems for practice.

One of the most incredible incidents happened as a result of the board's direction that the program was to be made available on a "first come first served" basis to all students and parents in the district. A registration date for the pilot program was set for a Saturday morning at 8 a.m. and was advertised to everyone in the district. At 12 p.m. the day before registration, the school board's president was seen with an umbrella, ice chest, and chair in line at the front of the registration office to enroll her child. Within a few hours, approximately 50 parents had joined her in line, including both the superintendent's wife and my wife who both had elementary children. Interestingly, the district employees were not given any priority for their own children to participate in the fundamental program. The school board insisted that everyone, as well as employees, stand in line if they wanted their children to participate in the program. I was confident and wanted to help support the program by including my own two children, so I called my wife and told her to get in line as quickly as possible.

By that evening more than 125 people were in line, all prepared for an overnight camp-out to help make sure their children were able to enroll in the pilot program. The day of registration 25 students in each of six classrooms in first through sixth grade, exceeding the district's student-to-teacher ratio. Not surprisingly, the situation created a significant "media buzz" from both the television and print media. By 10 a.m. on registration day more than 150 students were signed up for the pilot fundamental program to be held while the new school was being built. A waiting list was created to help assure that all students not selected for the pilot program could participate the following year after the new school construction project was completed. The parents were convinced the process was fair and those successful registrants were happy to have their children enrolled in the pilot fundamental program. There were no problems during the entire registration effort.

Besides local media coverage, the pilot program drew interest from many others in the state. The governor visited the district and was especially interested in the networked computer lab that was first tested at the oldest elementary school in the district. The State Superintendent of Public Education was in contact with the school and educators from districts all over the state came to visit.

Some of the teachers in the community and district were not happy with the fundamental school program. I believe some of the other teachers in the district felt the new school and its fundamental emphasis received too much attention from the administration. I also believe that many of the teachers and principals in other schools did not buy into the philosophy of the fundamental program. The overall instructional program was negatively viewed because of the emphasis on phonics in the reading program and the degree of instructional control from the administration. Although the initial fundamental teachers had requirements beyond others in the district, they may have been viewed as "favorites" of the administration.

I understand that veteran teachers might have preferred to work in a new facility, even though the new school addressed many aspects of elementary education differently. Not all the teachers chosen for the program were from the existing staff. The district was most interested in teachers supporting the school's fundamental nature. Change is difficult, especially from what was done in other schools. Many of the teachers did not understand why the fundamental program needed to be different. I understand why a teacher might wonder what was wrong with their existing program and why so many changes were needed for the new school? I am sure it was hard to accept the fact that the school attracted so many students, including children of the administration and school board.

The spring test results improved in all the district's schools that year. The fundamental school students performed better than all the other schools in the district and all the other schools in the community. Although I left the district after the first year of the pilot program, it is not surprising the climate in the district may have been less than optimal. The fundamental school was getting tremendously positive press and I am sure that was difficult for the staff at other schools. The teachers and administrators in the largest district in the community were concerned when the testing results were published because they were no longer had the best performance of the districts in the community!

While the initial ethnic demographics of the fundamental magnet school was closer to that of the other schools in the district, it is not surprising to see people use that as a reason the fundamental school had much better student performance. In building the program a major effort was made to include as many minority children as possible, especially those children with limited English-speaking skills. The district actively recruited Spanish-speaking students and held many Spanish meetings with minority parents. Since the program was offered on a first come first served basis, the district had no control over who chose to stand in line to get their children enrolled in the pilot program. The demographics of the school were likely more of an issue in years after the initial program was developed.

Throughout the years, many more Hispanic children moved into the community and the demographics in all of the schools in the area have changed significantly. However, we hoped the program (especially the reading and language arts program) would be accepted in the other schools and that the fundamental program would be more of a model for the other schools as well.

Although it will be discussed in more detail later, the emphasis on phonics and teaching the structure and code of the English language was especially helpful for the limited English-speaking children. I have always been interested in helping Spanish-speaking children succeed in school. My first five years as an administrator were in a school that served almost all Spanish-speaking students and my doctoral research dealt with the standardized testing of students by language ability.[24]

All of the fundamental magnet students were tested with the required state test in the late spring of the pilot first year. I believe publishing school performance data encourages administrators to be more conscious of student performance and the reputation of their school or district. School testing information should always be made available to parents. Within days of the publication of all the state testing results, an official at the State Department of Education contacted the administration of the fundamental district, notifying us an anonymous source had accused the fundamental pilot program teachers of cheating on the state test. The accusation was primarily directed at the fundamental school but included the entire district.

According to the state official that informed me of the complaint, it was impossible to have such a significant growth in student performance in one year without impropriety, especially in the fundamental school. In Arizona, such accusations, if accurate, are very serious and could result in the loss of teacher certification credentials. The district offered the State Department of Education the opportunity to administer a second test with another version of the same test to any or all the students in the pilot fundamental school. We hoped this would resolve the issue and deal with the complaint. The second version of the test covered the same skills as the first testing program. Even though there was no specific information besides the test results to indicate possible impropriety, the state department was told they could come at any time, without prior notice, and test any or all the students with the alternate test. The district did ask for at least one half-hour warning in order to plan for staff development activities during any state department testing effort.

The officials from the state department accepted the offer as a way to resolve and deal with the complaint, and traveled to the district unannounced and administered the second test to the fundamental school's first-graders. I was never told why they chose only to test the first-graders, but I am sure it would have been more expensive and difficult to retest the entire school. Although upset with the complaint we were convinced the students would perform well.

When the second testing was completed the State Superintendent of Education personally called to inform us that the school's first grade students who were tested performed even better than when the school's teachers first administered the test! The results were more incredible because the first grade classroom of 25 students included several limited English-speaking students. The entire situation resulted in a great deal of attention in the community and state.

The fact that the state's highest and most important educator personally called to inform us of their findings was not common. She told me she had never seen such significant academic progress in all her years in education. One comment especially made me happy. "Not one of your first-grade students missed any question on the Iowa Test of Basic Skills subtest measuring phonics. I would like you to come up to the State Department of Education and show us what you have done in your district to create such amazing academic achievement. I will make sure all our administrators are included in the meeting." We agreed on a date and presented the program to the state department officials. We were later told the State Superintendent of Education made some staff changes as a result of the situation. In her phone call, she told me, "It is not our practice to respond to anonymous complaints without specific information supporting such complaints." After the incident the State Superintendent of Education and governor of the state personally visited the district and became avid supporters of the program.

The development of specific time and subject recommendations was a key to the program's success. At the time my mother taught second grade in a neighboring district that was previously considered the best elementary school in the community (again based on excellent student performance.) Surprisingly, she asked for my help, even though she was inherently a confident and strong-willed teacher. She was a good teacher because she loved children and was concerned with student achievement. My mother told me that her second graders always had the best reading scores in her school, for which she was very proud (again using the state achievement test.) However, she related that her students fell down in mathematics performance as compared to the rest of the second graders in her school. I told her I would meet her one afternoon after school to see if I could help.

When I arrived at her classroom after her students were dismissed, her first comment was, "I love to teach reading but just hate math," which made me suspicious. I asked her to show me her typical teaching schedule. Her schedule emphasized reading but she taught math for a total of only one half-hour per day. I told her, "Mom, how do you expect your students to be successful in math if you spend most of your time teaching only the subjects you love most? Whether or not you don't like to teach math, you need to devote more time teaching math if your students are to be successful." She told me "Well, I could devote less time to art (which she loved) and increase math instruction." Not surprising, her math scores improved the following year. This experience further convinced me that most elementary schools do not have adequate control of instructional programming.

We asked the district's principals to impose teaching time allocations in their schools. It was not surprising that we experienced some resistance regarding the recommendations made by the district office. It became clear that other changes were needed in some of the other schools in the district. Eventually, some administrators retired or were simply non-renewed contractually. As one would assume, the level of tension rose among the staff, although many welcomed the changes.

In addition, a new emphasis was made on improving the overall quality of the teaching staff. A few teachers retired or were terminated, although an effort was made to help those individuals improve. I was very pleased that our efforts were successful. The superintendent developed a more formal teacher recruitment program. Several recruiting trips were made each year to find highly qualified teachers, particularly in special education areas. In all cases we were able to hire very capable teachers, often with multiple certifications and post-graduate degrees. The district provided all new teachers with training programs that outlined instructional expectations in hopes of helping improve classroom performance. In short, we were not convinced that the new teachers could implement instruction we wanted without additional training.

One of the concerns of the new school board was that the district also had a reputation for poor student behavior, including what some board members perceived as a drug problem. The district office developed a new discipline code that was subsequently approved by the school board. They addressed areas of classroom behavior, including appropriate dress and remedies to help eliminate any potential drug problem. At that time, we debated requiring student uniforms, which would have been the first school in the area to do so, but decided it would create too much controversy and eliminated the idea. Most of the elementary schools in the community now have uniforms. The fundamental school students would have been the first public school to require uniforms.

The administration made sure parents were involved in the development of the discipline code. The fundamental school parents were required to sign a form to acknowledge the discipline guidelines prior to each school year. The first test came several months later when some junior high school girls were caught selling penicillin pills as if they were amphetamine "speed" pills. All were reasonably good students and admitted their involvement but were suspended for the remainder of the school year as per the discipline code. Some parents appealed the suspension, but the school board upheld them.

One of the board members, a physician, noted that the buyers of the pills believed they were an amphetamine (speed) pills. He stated that some students might even have health complications with penicillin medications.

Every incident afterwards was dealt with according to the written discipline code. It became clear to parents and students that the district was going to enforce the new discipline guidelines.

Later in my career, I initiated a cooperative effort with law enforcement that provided drug-sniffing dogs for my schools. This helped with law enforcement training and made sure all students knew the district was serious about enforcing the discipline code as it related to illegal drugs. The effort further eliminated any potential drug issue in my schools. Some of the schools in the fundamental school community are now experiencing problems with several serious drug issues, including the highly dangerous drug fentanyl.

The fact that many of the schools have student resource officers (SROs) is very positive. I was fortunate to have worked with many outstanding SROs. I can't think of a better use of law enforcement than the SRO program, especially considering all the current nonsensical proposals to "defund the police." SRO programs are a perfect example of the effort to "reimagine policing efforts" and develop more "community policing." Without question, the SRO program has been a positive influence on America's students.

Rough Start for the Fundamental School

The students' achievement at the fundamental school was incredible! However, not long after the first incident another complaint was received from the Office of Civil Rights (OCR). The OCR told me the fundamental program was described as an "elitist" school consisting of too many non-minority students. In response to the complaint, we provided the OCR with the ethnic demographics of the school and district, as well as the documentation of the developmental meetings held with both Spanish-speaking minority and non-minority parents. The fundamental program had been made available to all parents. The district attempted to encourage the participation of minority children and we felt good about our efforts.

After reviewing the information we provided, the OCR dismissed the complaint. The identity of the complainant was never revealed. The school's academic performance was so good that the community took note. Frankly, I was very annoyed and tired of anonymous complaints!

The administration felt we could be able to adequately serve all the students, including learning disabled (LD) students. At that time, a learning disability label was given to students who were at least two academic levels behind their peers in reading or math. Additional intelligence testing was necessary for all of the learning disabled children in the district to determine which students had an average learning ability and actually qualified for services. However, we made sure the fundamental school parents understood that the pilot program could not provide formal special education services during initial stages. However, we assured parents all students would have the opportunity to receive extra tutoring before and after school in the resource program.

When the pilot program began at least 75 percent of the students participated in the resource program. Many of those students received extra support outside of classroom instruction. We were satisfied that this would alleviate any long-standing concern with regards to special services.

I would add that I believe far too many LD students are pulled out of instruction in the classroom to receive the same instruction in a resource room. It seems to me that students should receive additional instruction in deficient subjects. This system was a better fit for reading and language arts given the type of program we were using, which is something that will be discussed later in this book. I have always been concerned special education pullout programs make students feel different or inadequate.

At the registration for the pilot program, the parents were provided with all of the school's expectations. One such expectation included a parent/school requirement stating parents would have someone available to pick up students within 45 minutes if there was any type of problem, including sickness or behavior issues. Although I no longer have access to the statistics on behavior, I can't recall any student being sent home for behavioral issues in the pilot program. The students were always engaged and attentive even though the school hours were extended with the resource program, making it a long day for the students.

All the parents were required to sign the "parent contract" and the discipline code had complete support from the school community. The district had 100 percent cooperation with the entire effort in building the fundamental school program. I have never worked in any situation where parent cooperation and involvement was better than the fundamental school.

Every teacher personally made a home visit to meet with their students and parents when the fundamental school parents completed the registration process prior to the first day of school. Each visit lasted approximately one hour, during which time the program was discussed. All parents were briefed on program expectations that included the basics of student management. The fact that the teachers took the time to visit with their future students created even more excitement for the program. "The concept of classroom management is broader than the notion of student discipline. It includes all the things teachers must do to foster student involvement and cooperation in classroom activities and to establish a productive work environment."[25]

The fundamental teachers attempted to place more emphasis on positive student behaviors rather than trying to control unproductive behaviors. A major problem in most classrooms is the instructional time that is wasted by teachers having to deal with discipline issues. Such was not the case with the fundamental program. There were few problems with behavior. The fundamental teachers attempted to create strong positive student-teacher relationships. Research clearly shows that academic achievement and student behavior are highly influenced by the quality of student and teacher relationships.[26] All of the fundamental teachers attempted to create these high-quality, strong, positive student-teacher relationships.

New teachers are influenced by what happens in other classrooms and what other teachers are doing or certainly what they may have been taught in university teacher training programs. Although I am currently retired, I continue to be involved in classroom visitations, some as a substitute teacher in districts that cannot get substitutes. I believe many off-task behaviors in elementary classrooms result from poor classroom organization. I attended a parochial school, and at the risk of sounding older than dirt, I enjoyed having my own desk as a young student. I could keep my books and other materials in my desk and took pride in neatness. The teachers arranged the desks in a basic fashion, usually in rows. This allowed for clear view of the teacher whose desk and instructional supplemental equipment was situated at the front of the room.

Many elementary teachers have changed the manner in which student furniture is arranged. Some teachers have student desks pushed together in a multitude of arrangement schemes. Multiple groups of students sit at tables or at desks that are grouped together. This type of furniture arrangement can result in off-task behaviors. As I remember my days in school, I was less attentive if I sat close to other students, especially if they were close friends. Such is the case with many public school classrooms. Students should always be able to see their teacher and vice versa. The teacher should never have their backs to the students. Tables should only be used if a small group of students are working on some type of cooperative activity and directly controlled. Teachers should be encouraged to circulate around the classroom and make as much direct contact as possible. I am suspicious when I see a teacher sitting down during instruction time. The fundamental classrooms were quiet and controlled. I rarely heard more than one student talking at a time.

I was recently perusing boxes of pictures and memorabilia and found a report card from my father's "primer" class in Pittsburgh, Kansas. I discovered he attended St. Mary's School, a Catholic parochial school. I was especially interested to see his report card that, in addition to Christian doctrine, he was graded in spelling, reading, writing, and arithmetic (and numbers), as well as application, neatness, and deportment (basically behaving according to the student behavior code).

I was surprised by my own sixth-grade parochial school report card. Besides religion as a subject, I received grades in English, reading, spelling, history, civics, arithmetic, and science. In addition, I was also graded in penmanship, music, and art, as well as conduct and effort. The worst grade I received was a C in conduct. As I recall, I did not like my sixth-grade teacher and the poor conduct grade I received was likely influenced by my feelings about that teacher. I was surprised because I thought I had always been a good student, but my behavior was apparently not very good. The point is that, perhaps we are missing something that could improve our current grading systems, particularly in the elementary grades.

A student's ability to succeed is correlated with conduct and effort. Why not incorporate some traditional approaches to evaluating student performance and include conduct and effort?

As you can imagine, the first year for the new school board and administration was difficult. While we were very proud of student performance, the situation created increased tensions, particularly with the employees of neighboring districts. More parents wanted to move into our district and we began to see realtors advertising "homes for sale located in our district" and "walking distance to the fundamental school."

When the district built the new fundamental school, the contractor building new homes close to the school couldn't build homes fast enough. Many years later, I had a chance to talk with that contractor who had been very vocal in opposing the termination of his friend, the former superintendent. He was very gracious and told me, "The new elementary fundamental school was the most important thing that helped me build so many homes. I was wrong in thinking the whole idea of the new school was stupid and would hurt my company. In retrospect it helped my business boom and I sincerely thank you." That was one of the most rewarding conversations I've had in my life, and something I will never forget, especially since he passed away shortly after that. The process of change and improvement can be stressful. Making any type of major change in a school program can be very difficult!

In the first year, the new school board and administration had to address other issues in the district. They began the new school year with a formal complaint from the Office of Civil Rights (OCR). The complaint was legitimate in that previously poorly performing limited and non-English speaking students were routinely assigned to special education and given learning-disabled labels. The previous administration approved this placement because there was no other program available to deal with their English language deficiencies.

No student should ever be given a special education label simply because of a language deficiency.

The district was able to resolve the complaint by hiring another school psychologist and retesting every student in the district who had previously been identified as learning disabled, thus modifying the entire special education program. The district also built a program to serve limited and non-English speaking children. Having had almost 40 years in administration I have yet to see such a lengthy complaint, threatening the issuance of all federal assistance to the district. Testing every special education student was very time-consuming and expensive. The district's effort to deal with the complaint was approved by the OCR and the administration received documentation that all issues had been addressed appropriately, resolving the complaint.

That program, as well as other programs in the district, won many awards from the Arizona School Boards and National School Boards Associations. If districts took those recommendations of *A Nation At Risk* and addressed them in the development of their programs, the educational system in America would again rank among the best in the world. After the new program was operational, the following letter was received from T.H. Bell, President Reagan's Secretary of Education.

Dear Dr. Dallabetta:

I was pleased to hear about the new special education program you are starting and the new school you are opening. I am happy to return the posters you sent, which have been autographed by the President.

In striving to implement the recommendations of the National Commission on Excellence in Education, I wish you every success in preparing your students for the challenging future ahead. To your students I would add a word of encouragement in their studies: Work hard, study intensely, learn well. No matter what future you prepare for, live and work so that you will make your dreams a reality and make your mark on the world.

Thank you for telling me about your program. I hope you enjoy your posters.

Sincerely,

T. H. Bell, United States Secretary of Education

Special Education in the Fundamental School

The use of the term *special education* in Bell's letter did not refer to formal special education programs for children with established handicaps. It was intended to reference the fact that the new school's philosophy was unique and consisted of a very effective instructional program.

In the initial pilot year, the fundamental school did not officially serve special education students. The children who registered for the program carrying the learning disabled (LD) label received extra help before and after school in the resource program. Parents of the LD children eagerly signed waivers for formal special education services. Not surprisingly, those students functioned well and showed tremendous academic growth. This outcome was the result of extra instructional assistance and the nature of the program.

The assignment of special education labels is a serious matter. In my experience, students classified as LD often remain in special education programs for years, making me suspicious of the effectiveness of such programs.

The elementary school in Texas attended by my youngest grandson recently requested a meeting with his parents. In the meeting they told his parents that my grandson was having difficulty in reading although they stated that he was "very smart." After gaining approval from his parents, the school tested him and requested another meeting to ask for parent approval to provide special education programming since testing had determined that my grandson was dyslexic, a disturbance of the ability to read.

When discussing the situation with my daughter and her husband, I reminded them of the program in which she participated in the fundamental program. She was concerned that her son's problems with reading may have resulted from a lack of proper instruction in his first three grades, particularly with the lack of phonics instruction in the school's reading program. They decided that they would not approve of any special education label for their son. I believe they made the right decision. They are extremely active as parent volunteers and aware of the lack of phonics instruction in the primary grades at their son's school. In the interim, they hired their own tutor to address his lack of phonetic skills and, not surprisingly, his reading skills continued to improve. One of the school's administrators told my daughter she thought that the school would address the lack of phonics instruction in the next school year. Too little too late and to this day nothing has significantly been changed in the school!

Eliminating the Fundamental School

Sadly, years later, new district superintendents and school board members abandoned the fundamental school philosophy and program. I was horrified when I looked at the current performance of the students. The fact that the district had eliminated such a successful program really bothered me, especially considering the tremendous effort and research that went into building the fundamental school. After returning to the community many years after the fundamental program had been eliminated, I formally requested the school district governing board drop the word *fundamental* from the school's name. Successive administrations have all but eliminated the phonics-based reading program and most of the important components of the original program. It was no longer a fundamental school. As a result, I sent the following letter to all members of the current governing board.

February 3, 2018

Members of the School District Governing Board:

Firstly, I would like to thank you for your efforts to serve the students, staff, and constituents of the district. Your job is not easy but so critical in helping our children get the best possible public education. I would like you to consider a fairly simple action that would, in my opinion, enhance the integrity of the district and, in particular, the former fundamental school. (Please note that I have chosen to eliminate reference to any specific individual.)

It is my sincere belief that it is important to remove the term "fundamental" from the former elementary school. Having worked for over a year with parents and the Governing Board to develop the original concept for the creation of the magnet program we addressed many philosophical issues critical in establishing what could honestly be labeled a fundamental program. Although there were many issues addressed in the original effort, they included mandatory parental involvement and an instructional program that emphasized an integrated reading and writing program with attention to the most important basic skills. Originally the parents opted out of a lunch program and transportation services in order to fund a wonderful before and after school resource program. Having worked with school budgets for over 30 years it is important to note that food service and transportation program can create additional funds for many districts, which, in this case, funded the resource program. The school was also built with a science lab and one of the first networked computer labs in an American elementary school. The dedication of the teachers that received special training and the students to carefully utilize time on task efforts created the highest performing school in the community as well as one of the best performing elementary school in the State of Arizona. Amazingly, parents whose children were labeled as learning disabled, formally opted out of special education services because they were not needed given the strength of the program. Attention to American history, government, and in particular patriotism honored perhaps one of the greatest Presidents to ever serve our country.

The basic documentary principles supporting the foundation of the school are now housed in a Presidential Library. For that reason and as a result of the changes made over the years I believe it is not accurate to use the term "fundamental" on the school's sign that, in my opinion, creates a credibility issue for the school and district. If public schools would provide strong marketable programs that parents want, there would never be a need for charter schools, which have now saturated our community. Further, there would never be a need to advertise commercially to compete for student enrollment.

In closing, I would be happy to further explain the many differences between most contemporary public elementary schools and the former elementary school as a fundamental magnet program, so popular that many parents camped out to enroll on a first come first served basis. These parents included those of both limited English speaking and learning disabled children. As the person responsible for creating the program I would be happy to provide specific information of what I have described in this letter. Lastly, I would ask the proposal in this letter be included as an action item at a future Board meeting. Thank you again for serving the students and I look forward to a response to this proposal.

Sincerely yours,

Patrick M. Dallabetta

The current governing board, supported by the superintendent, voted unanimously to accept my recommendation and agreed to drop the term *fundamental* from the school's name. They also removed *fundamental* from the sign in front of the school but never took me up on my offer to discuss the reasons the school was so successful.

According to the local newspaper quoting a current district administrator, "Through the years, the school has changed significantly, the district said, and the word 'fundamental' no longer defines the school which today is innovative, technology-focused and embeds the arts." There was actually no information provided that explained the description of the current program.

The district superintendent made a personal call to me verifying that the governing board would honor my recommendation. I appreciated her phone call to discuss the vote. The fact that the superintendent called me was very professional. The superintendent later told the local newspaper "the elementary school will be dropping the 'fundamental' from its name, as the school is no longer a magnet campus for teaching the basics."

What is wrong with focusing on the basics? Since the superintendent has stated the school is innovative and technology-focused, someone should ask why the children in the current school are performing so poorly?

The information on the district's website states the district has math and reading proficiency scores that exceed the state average. In real figures they exceed the state average by only 1 percent and if parents really understood the information provided, the district's scores are worse than 57 percent of the total schools in Arizona, a state that already has poor student achievement.[27]

The fundamental school was eliminated for reasons I will likely never understand. I do know successive superintendents and some teachers were not apparently vested in the philosophy of the program and I even heard the fundamental school was referred to as an "elitist school for the district's Mormon students." (The former president of the district governing board was a member of the

Church of Jesus Christ Latter-Day Saints.) That is one of the most unfair comments I have ever heard.

Successive superintendents of the district have been popular with the staff of the district. Popularity with teachers and the teacher's association or teacher's union will certainly enhance the tenure of any school administrator. Teachers place great importance on influencing the decisions made by school districts' governing boards. Could this have been the main source in the effort to eliminate the school? There was certainly a fair amount of critics of the school among the staff who were not participants in the program.

The current student scores in the now-defunct fundamental school are poor and sad to me as a former administrator of such a formerly successful program. How could district's governing board allow such a travesty to happen and did employee influences in the district's other schools provide the basis for the decision to eliminate the school?

Science, Technology, Engineering, and Math (STEM)

Many years after the fundamental program was eliminated, the current administration of the district fundamental school has implemented the Science, Technology, Engineering, and Math (STEM) Program.[28] It began essentially as a magnet program and was named and supported by one of the community's most prestigious philanthropists. STEM programs integrate the four curriculum areas describe in the acronym and creates a student-centered program of study. The STEM magnet program has become very popular with parents living in and outside the district for a very good reason. Student performance in the program leads all the schools in the community and has received an A rating by the state. The school ranks first in the community and district, and is among the 100 best ranked schools in Arizona. Their science scores are incredible and reading and math scores are well above average as compared to other schools in the district.

The fact that the current district STEM ranked 96th of the 1,029 schools in Arizona is very impressive. To be included in the top one hundred schools in Arizona is a tremendous accomplishment. If I were an administrator in the area, I would be very interested to know why the STEM program is so successful. This would certainly influence the strategies to improve any school's rank. It is likely other districts and schools in the area will be influenced to adopt STEM programming.

If the fundamental school was eliminated because of the racial-ethnic imbalance, the current district has a similar problem. The racial ethnic demographics of the original fundamental school in its first year were only slightly different from the school district. I have been told the fundamental school was eliminated in part because of a skewed racial-ethnic breakdown. This may be true considering the changes in the ethnic makeup of the district over the years. Ironically, neither does the racial-ethnic breakdown of the district's first STEM school.

Using the 2020 statistics, 48.7 percent of the STEM students are Hispanic with another 47.1 percent of the students listed as white or not specified. In contrast to these figures, minority enrollment in the district is 87 percent minority, well above the Arizona average of 62 percent minority students.[29] If the fundamental school were eliminated because of a skewed percentage of non-minority children, I would think the district still has a problem with the racial-ethnic issue in their new STEM magnet program.

The STEM program achievement scores are much better in comparison to other schools in the district, a fact that is very meaningful as an individual school accomplishment. According to the Public School Review website, the school ranks in the top 10 percent of schools in the state in both reading and math proficiency.[30] However, the fact that only one of 13 total schools is doing well does not mean the district is excelling.

In reality, overall district math and reading proficiency has dropped since 2014 and does not even come close to the achievement test scores of the original fundamental school. Only 39 percent of elementary and 29 percent of middle school students are proficient in math and 42 percent of elementary school students and 31 percent of middle school students are proficient in reading, statistics that are not impressive.[31] The Public School Review website rates the district as being in the bottom 50 percent of schools in the state. However, the district claims its student academic performance is within the top 50 percent of districts in the state.

The performance of the former fundamental school, once among the top performers in the state, has plummeted. In 2017 only 38 percent of the school's students passed the state's mandated test in reading with only 49 percent of the students passing the mathematics portion of the test. In 2018, there was no improvement in reading and the percentage of students passing the mathematics portion of the test dropped to 42 percent, a decrease of 7 percent points.[32]

In contrast, during the first year of the fundamental school program, students scored in the 96th percentile on the state's reading test and were among the best state scores in both language arts and mathematics. Although the state-mandated test has changed over the years, it is safe to say that the original program was an incredible success story!

Why eliminate something that was so successful? Why not build on the philosophy of providing special programming and more choices for all the district's constituents?

According to the website SchoolDigger.com the former fundamental school now ranks 717 of of 1,029 Arizona Elementary Schools.[33] The SchoolDigger.com statistics are derived from the National Center for Education, the U.S. Department of Education, the U.S. Census Bureau, and the Arizona Department of Education (also available on education department websites of other states in the U.S.).

The decline in test scores may be at least partially attributed to the increased enrollment numbers of limited English-speaking children and the racial-ethnic differences in the school's students since the original school program was developed. Almost 87 percent of the school's current students are minority children. However, the current challenges for the district's elementary program could be better addressed by adopting a program that serves these students, including a systematic phonics program to help the children learn to speak, read, and write English. The students' performance would certainly improve by using the strategies and programs of the former fundamental school.

The district should provide a phonics-based reading program and more allocated instruction time, particularly in reading and language arts. I believe it is far easier to create better academic growth when you are dealing with non-English or limited English-speaking students, especially if you have a strong instructional program.

Several years ago, I was contracted to help an elementary school in central Phoenix. The students in the school were predominantly Hispanic, similar to the schools in the fundamental school district. At that time, the State Department of Education ranked schools with labels ranging from "highly performing to failing." The school I was contracted to help was very close to being given a failing label. Just one year later, after more effort in tracking students' individual performance and adding more instruction time, the school was given a rating of "performing plus." The positive change was due to efforts to carefully examine the academic performance of each student, work to control the instructional program, and increase the allocated instruction for the underperforming students.

Several school districts in the metropolitan Phoenix area have established what they term basic or traditional schools, all of which produce excellent student performance and are very popular with parents. Many of these schools allow parents living outside attendance boundaries to participate in their programs, making them true magnet schools.

School districts that offer more choices and provide special academic programs are generally more successful in producing higher student achievement, a situation that seems to positively correlate with parent satisfaction.

Historically Personal Problems!

My own family has had issues with our children and public schools. Some of these problems are the result of ignorance or, worse yet, stupidity. Regardless, I am lucky to have grandchildren who are doing well in school. Their performance is partially a result of supportive parents who have established very high expectations for their children.

Despite superior performance, my youngest daughter's high school advanced English teacher refused to give her the higher grade we felt she had earned which kept her from achieving higher graduation accolades. The teacher's reasoning was that my daughter did not qualify to be in the advanced class in the first place because she had not been identified or labeled as a gifted student. Her initial placement in the advanced class was only a result of her former high performance as a student. Had she been formally identified as a gifted child it would not likely have been as much of an issue to the teacher. Unfortunately, her teacher made it clear to the principal that she did not like me as the superintendent, a situation I feel may have influenced her treatment of my daughter. Another disgruntled teacher gave her a B in band because of what he felt was bad posture. What?

My children had some great teachers and, unfortunately, a few very poor teachers. One of my high school grandchildren was assigned to lead a small group of students to complete a "cooperative learning project." His group peers did not complete their respective assignments. As a result, the other students received failing grades for the project. The teacher, knowing my grandson did most of the work, gave him a grade of B, which eliminated him from the possibility of higher academic honors at his high school graduation ceremony. She openly commented that his work was excellent but lowered his grade despite the fact that he had done the work for the other students.

Another grandson excelled in eight years of elementary school. He enrolled in a parochial high school with a reputation for excellence and high standards. His performance the first year was poor, a situation new to our family. But, as the counselor said, "He is simply not ready for the rigors of our school." I have no doubt the counselor was right but how could this happen? What happened in his elementary school years where he was an outstanding student? He has since adapted and become a very good college student.

My only granddaughter, a highly skilled national class twirler, marched with her high school band her first year of high school. However, she was not allowed to participate in the second semester concert band because she did not play an instrument in the marching band. Why would the teacher not allow this young lady to continue with her music education just because she chose to twirl rather than play her instrument in the marching band? She was a former first chair saxophone player in middle school. Sadly, she no longer plays her instrument or participates in any instrumental music programs. However, she is a freshman twirler in a large university marching band.

In another district, I overturned the high school principal's decision not to allow a very talented gymnast an early release from high school for her training regimen. This young lady, only a freshman, was the best student in the entire school but was required to physically train at least four hours a day. The principal was worried that other students might ask to be released from school early and that releasing any student would set a precedent for other requests. I intervened in an appeal from the parents and believed her situation was unique. She was a national class gymnast, already able to compete at any major college even though she was only a high school freshman. That, in addition to her academic performance in high school, justified an early release. I created an appeal process to address future requests for early release.

Some of my grandchildren generally have poor, illegible written skills, as it seems penmanship instruction is no longer important in elementary schools. They may be able to type messages on their cell phones or even have fair keyboarding skills, but they have trouble writing legibly. So, when did penmanship no longer become important in our elementary schools? How could elementary education abandon something so basic as penmanship, especially considering the relationship to reading and writing?

My wife and I recently attended a movie, and we were surprised to see local districts advertising for students, likely due to the increasing interest in charter school programs throughout the community. In most states, the primary funding support is based on full-time equivalency

(FTE). Therefore, formally advertising programs is one of several strategies districts use to build student enrollment. Most parents are willing to do whatever is needed to enroll their children in the best schools. Advertising expenditures could be better used to develop more effective and popular programs.

In the early 90's, the issue of allowing children to enroll in charter schools at public expense became a big issue with public school educators. They don't like losing state financial support allocated for the education of its public school students. However, parents deserve a choice, and the former fundamental school community is now saturated with charter schools and even parochial school enrollment is growing. The public school districts in the state are losing thousands of students to charter or private school programs.

Instead of having to advertise for students, why not try to develop programs to attract more students?

Chapter 4

PARENTS: LOOK AT YOUR SCHOOL'S PERFORMANCE

The first step in choosing a school for your children is to carefully examine student performance at schools being considered. All the information you need is easily accessible on the Internet. There are many websites that provide excellent information about all schools. Most importantly, they provide helpful information about students' performance in schools. A first step should be to access performance data from your State Department of Education. Some of the research in this book came from the Arizona Department of Education and SchoolDigger.com websites. Any of the following websites may be especially helpful to parents.

https://schooldigger.com
https://niche.com
https://nces.ed.gov
https://greatschools.org
https://fraserinstitue.org
https://usnews.com
https://publiccharters.org

Test scores are also available for charter schools. While the overall performance of charter school students may be a little better than those in public schools, parents should consider all factors in considering which schools they choose for their children.

My own daughter carefully looked at one of the best charter school programs in her state before registering her children in her local public high school. Her concern was, "My children are very involved in athletics. While producing great test scores, the charter school was not a good option for my children because their emphasis was to study, study, and study." All of her children eventually received college academic scholarships and were all college athletes.

The NICHE.com provides another quick method for parents to examine school ratings.[34] The NICHE website provides a map to reference the location of schools. The information included on the website contains overall NICHE grades (originating from state's education department assessments), ethnic statistics, and grade ratings for the schools' teachers (likely established by certification information.)

According to NICHE.com, their purpose is to help "Find the right school for your child." It allows you to view up to four schools at a time and examine key factors such as academic quality, diversity, teacher quality, student-teacher ratio, and school size. NICHE.com allows parents to create an account to customize the attributes you compare and begin to build a list of schools to research. Their comparisons include information for the public, private, charter, and magnet schools.

It is interesting that I used NICHE.com to search for the best elementary school in my community. The search revealed no schools in my current location are rated highly, given the attributes I provided in their questionnaire!

Chapter 5

TARGETING LOWER PERFORMING STUDENTS AND SPECIAL EDUCATION

The foundation of American education is built on somewhat of a philosophic misnomer. We spend a huge amount of our resources and time teaching to what has been called the "lower quartiles." In the United States we focus on compensatory education, trying to help failing students. Students with more capacity, desire, and potential to succeed are often left to fend for themselves.

I have spent most of my time in public school administration and clearly understand the education budget process. During my 37 years, schools have been required by law or regulation to spend a large portion of their fiscal resources on students lagging in achievement. That is what we do in American education and it is very important.

Unfortunately, the philosophy of "No Child Left Behind" emphasized in the Bush administration, may be ideological craziness. Don't get me wrong. We must do whatever we can to help all students succeed. But I've got some news for you. It is just plain nuts to think we can make every student successful. Before you think I am totally "wacked," let me give you a few specific examples.

The United States has been overwhelmed by incredible numbers of children who are newly immigrated or whose parents have crossed our southern border illegally. According to television media information from both the U.S. Border Patrol and Custom and Immigration officials, the children of parents come from over 100 different countries. While most of the children are Spanish speakers, we have numerous other children who are non-English speakers of many different languages. Schools are required to provide an education to all of those students because they are residing in an American school district. It is hard to imagine the difficulty schools have in dealing with so many foreign language speakers. The fact that they end up locating in an American school district or school attendance zone entitles them a free and appropriate education.

You do not have to be a citizen to be entitled to an education in America. You simply have to be a resident of the district, legal or not. Consequently, our schools must create untold compensatory programs to deal with those students. It is frightening to think how much of our educational resources are spent in an effort to properly educate all such students.

Our country is the greatest, and I can understand why people want to relocate to the United States. But is it fair for American schools to spend such a huge amount of their resources to create so many compensatory programs for noncitizens?

American educational institutions spend enormous amounts of money educating handicapped children. Federal and state governments require them to do so and provide additional funding for special programs (although the resources they provide are not even close to the actual costs of programming).

Having overseen special education in several districts I can tell you that what is required of our special education system is hurting teachers' ability to teach effectively. Teachers are overburdened with paperwork and meeting deadlines so much that the amount of time they can spend with children is negatively impacted. While it is important to do our best to educate children who need help, we are wasting millions of dollars.

I recall one specific case of a newly immigrated student (not a US citizen but a resident of the district) enrolled in my unified district. That 20 1/2 year-old student was among the most handicapped students I have ever seen. The student was blind, deaf, very physically disabled, and had many of the most severe issues I have ever seen in any student. This was clearly a student who had absolutely no chance of succeeding. Yet our public school was required to serve this new immigrant special education student until he reached his 21st birthday, only six months from his registration date. That situation has since changed because a federal judge ruled that schools must serve special education students through the school year of their twenty-first birthday or until they reach the age of twenty-two.

This student required a specially certified school psychologist to test him because he was so severely handicapped. He had his own occupational and physical therapists to address his small and gross motor skills, his own speech pathologist, a hearing-impaired teacher, his own teacher aide (because he required one-on-one attention), and his own special education teacher who was required to have special credentials to serve this uniquely disabled student. The costs to educate this student did not include the tremendous amount of time that teachers, specialists, and administrators spent helping develop his individual education plan (IEP) and formally placing him in special education. His most important IEP goal was to pick up a piece of food and put it in his mouth without help. He never mastered that skill.

In the one semester the district was required to serve this student, it spent well over $50,000 "educating" a clearly "uneducable" student. It is important to serve handicapped students, but that same large school district had a total budget of only $5,000 allocated to serve its "gifted" students. The money we spent could have been better utilized on remedial programs for other students who needed more help and had the ability to learn. Perhaps it could have been used to provide a calculus or Latin class for high school students capable of that level of study. I don't believe we are doing enough to support students who either achieve at high levels or are academically gifted. The situation I described illustrates the power of the special education lobby.

Chapter 6

LEARNING DISABILITY LABELS AND SPECIAL EDUCATION

Students who carry a learning-disabled label require special services by state and federal law. I am especially supportive of remedial programs to help our children succeed. However, I do not support the need to give children a special education label if it can be avoided. This is especially important if you consider why children are identified as learning-disabled. Generally, a student of average ability (as determined by intelligence testing) qualifies for services as a learning-disabled student if they are at least two grade levels behind their peers in academic performance in reading or math. I completely support more intensive assistance for students but believe many learning difficulties result from poor instruction in early school years.

The research and work of Dr. Hilde L. Mosse should be required in all elementary teacher-training programs. *The Complete Handbook of Children's Reading Disorders*[35] is an incredible publication. Dr. Mosse is a former pediatrician who specialized in child and adolescent psychiatry. The purpose of her work was to describe how careful clinical examination of children disentangles all the different factors involved in the causation of reading disorders. Dr. Mosse is very supportive of programs that provide a multisensory approach to reading instruction and integrates reading instruction and phonics with writing and penmanship. If teachers were to utilize her work in reading instruction, there would likely be little need to give a child a learning-disabled label in reading.

The effort required to document that handicapped students receive a "free and appropriate" education according to required regulations necessitates an absolute insane amount of time and paperwork. States regularly audit the files of handicapped students. Any minor discrepancy in guidelines results in a written deficiency statement. Too many deficiencies in a special education audit can put state and federal funding at risk.

If you were to truly understand the burdens we have placed on our teachers to document the "learning process," you would understand that they have a difficult time teaching because we have "handicapped" them with a bureaucratic process that is incredibly time-consuming.

Many parents of special needs children want their children to be educated in the "mainstream" with other children, a situation I understand. However, providing the opportunity to educate some handicapped students in the mainstream can create problems.

In one school, the parents of a handicapped student requested that their child be taught in the regular classroom (mainstreamed) during the entire instructional day. While we tried to do our best, that particular student was a danger to the other students. He routinely physically hurt other students, became easily outraged, screamed, and even exposed himself to the children in the classroom.

The district eventually refused to allow the child complete mainstreaming and the parents filed a formal complaint with the state accusing the district of not providing a "free appropriate education." After a lot of time and legal resources, the district prevailed in the situation and the child was removed from the classroom. The district did attempt to include him in as many mainstream activities as appropriate. However, the student was never successfully controlled in any situation where interaction with other students was required!

Chapter 7

WHAT IS IMPORTANT IN AN EDUCATIONAL PROGRAM?

The two ingredients essential to effective instruction include both the quality and quantity of instruction. A bureaucracy that demands so much paperwork (kill as many trees as possible) is decimating what limited time we have to help students become properly educated human beings. The system has mandated that we prove performance by keeping records and scheduling countless meetings. Whether or not a student is successful doesn't seem to matter as much as keeping proper paperwork.

Schools need to increase the amount of available instruction time. The school day should be long enough to allow more students the opportunity to master essential skills. Clearly some countries understand this basic premise and have longer school calendars or school days, which is just one reason we are getting our butts kicked in terms of general performance. Your value as an educator in those countries is often based on your ability to produce positive outcomes in student achievement.

Give our teachers the time they need to teach. Research has clearly proven that it takes some students more time to master individual skills. So, we must cherish instruction time and eliminate wasted time. I cannot begin to describe how much time is wasted during the instructional day, especially with activities that may have little educational value. I can assure you that teachers must better utilize the time they have to teach, having visited hundreds of classrooms.

Students learn at their own individual pace. So let them do so by creating a system that allows students to move ahead as they are capable.

As a brand new principal, I once had to deal with an outraged group of fifth-grade teachers who were upset at their school's fourth-grade teachers because they were using the fifth-grade reading materials for some of the more advanced students as early as March in the school year. They claimed it was unprofessional because "Some of the fourth-grade students will have already been taught some of the fifth-grade skills in our instructional program, so what are we supposed to do?" It didn't help my popularity by saying "Perhaps some of the fifth-grade students may be ready to move into the sixth-grade materials early!" What is wrong with an advanced first-grade student being taught second-grade skills if they are ready?

I will never forget one kindergarten student I had in my first administrative assignment. On the first day of school, she did not want to play with the other children at recess and seemed happier sitting on the floor with a book in the hall next to the exit door to the playground. I sat down on the floor with her and asked why she didn't want to play with the other children. She told me she had more fun reading during recess. I was curious and asked her what she was reading, as she was just five years old. She showed me her book, *Little Women.* This little girl was so far advanced! I met with her teacher and arranged for her to participate in some advanced activities. I was lucky to have noticed her so early in the school year and so pleased that she was assigned to a fabulous first grade teacher. That teacher was able to accommodate her instructional abilities.

I think it is a good thing that our current educational systems seem focused more on the quality aspect of teaching. The best possible teachers can create better learning. Speaking of quality, how can we expect to maintain the best possible teachers when everyone knows teachers must be willing to accept lower wages in comparison to many college graduates in other fields? Although the situation is improving, you must love teaching to accept some teacher salaries.

I've heard the argument that our teachers get more vacations than most. But I would be willing to bet that most teachers would be happy to accept much less time off if they could get a better wage and be paid better for their efforts. Teachers usually need to further their education to move on salary schedules by enrolling in summer school.

I went to summer school every year for nine years, paid my own tuition, and supported my family by working at a gas station while I went to summer school full-time. The irony of my situation was that I made more money selling tires in two and a half months during the summer than I did the entire school year as a new teacher.

In theory, better teacher salaries should attract more capable teachers. It also seems plausible the money districts spend on education should correlate highly with the best student performance. However, there is a huge difference between states in the total per-pupil expenditures for education.

The New York per-pupil expenditures in the 2016 Annual Survey of School System Finances were $22,366 while Utah per-pupil expenditures in the same year was $6,953. Yet New York was ranked 25th for pre-kindergarten to 12th grade performance while Utah was ranked 22nd in the same survey.[36] Their survey added additional qualities of health care, education, and infrastructure in states, as well as their economies and quality of life.

In comparing teachers' salaries, New York was the clear winner with an average estimated teacher salary of $85,889. At that time when Utah teachers averaged $50,342. Many other factors are involved in estimates, such as benefits, pension costs, and other important variables such as living costs.

The large variation in teacher salaries seems to support the argument that the costs of education and quality of education are not necessarily correlated. This argument will certainly be ongoing for years to come.

Although I have recently seen progress in addressing teacher salary programs, competitive salaries for teachers continue to be inadequate. I do recognize the efforts school districts have begun to improve teacher salaries. However, I would argue that something must be done to attract our brightest college graduates, scientists, and mathematicians to the teaching profession if we are to succeed as a nation. I have heard many politicians talk about how the future of a nation depends on its educational system, yet little has recently been done to address poor performance issues in our country.

Detailed records are required to ensure teachers are teaching the correct sequence of basic skills. I think more consistent and systematic teaching is a good thing, but do so without sentencing our teachers to "death by paperwork." Regardless, this brings me to a situation I consider a problem. Every state finds it necessary to create its own test to help make sure to measure student performance. While testing is very important, if our children are to demonstrate academic progress, what makes anyone think that it is a good thing to have each state do their own thing when it comes to testing?

As an example, in Arizona, it was at one time the AzMerit test, in California the STAR test, and the list goes on and on, often changing far too often in each state. I believe that most states are testing most of the same important basic skills, so why not have one national test administered to all students in all states? This would allow for more objective analysis because every student would be tested by one standard. This would also help teachers deal with a very mobile student population. I clearly understand the concept of local control and have no expectations that this would ever become a reality.

Perhaps we should implement a testing program that necessitates competencies at third, sixth, eighth grades, and secondary schools. While this has merit, competency requirements will likely never happen even though it is a common practice in the educational systems of other and more successful countries.

The mobility rate was about 40 percent in one elementary school I worked. I wish someone could explain to me how to properly track performance in the absence of a common standard with such high student mobility! Of course, this would require all of our states to agree on the specific testing objectives to be included in a national test. The effort to develop a national test of basic skills will certainly continue to be unsuccessful, especially given the bipartisan political nature of our country. In my schools, we tried to test all new and transfer students to determine their academic status, while attempting to establish a base of instructional needs. This seemed the best thing to do, but required an incredible amount of time from our teachers.

Our teachers must spend far too much time dealing with students who do not have the desire to learn.

It is crazy to hear all the different special education labels used to describe student misbehavior. Students who want to succeed lose valuable instruction as the teachers waste time dealing with misbehavior. The situation has worsened in the past 50 years. The educational community should provide alternatives for students who constantly cause classroom disruptions.

I cannot properly discuss the degradation of American education without comments about parents and their influence on student success in school. As a young man I was expected to behave and do well in school. I was taught that a good education was a path to success in life. I don't think my own children ever thought their formal public education ended in 12th grade. In high school they knew they would go to college. The only dilemma they faced was choosing what college to attend and what program to study.

Parents must teach children at an early age that school is important, and they must succeed. Good students have parents who are involved and expect their children to behave and succeed in school. They don't make excuses for children and are willing to spend time helping them achieve.

My own family is average in every respect, yet all have achieved at very high levels in elementary, secondary, and college programs. They knew their parents cared and that it was important to do well in school. The four people in my family have ten college degrees.

Children who achieve at higher levels have been taught that school is a very important opportunity. But let's face it, not every student is going to go to college, let alone become literate. Many of those students have no desire to succeed in school. Unfortunately, a few students see school as a place to have fun and often seem satisfied creating chaos. Those students must be offered a choice. Behave and show some effort or be removed. Perhaps they need more practical vocational programming or a special school that has the capability to focus on behavior issues. Regardless, the American education system needs to understand how important it is to remove disruptive students from the mainstream so that our teachers can teach and students who appreciate the importance of education have the ability and opportunity to learn.

Remember the "old days" when students (especially in parochial schools) received two different grades for each subject. One grade represented progress in each area of instruction and the other was an appraisal of the student's conduct, behavior, and effort.

Some of our teacher training institutions don't teach how to properly manage classrooms or deal with disciplinary issues. I did not have any college class that taught me how to deal with disruptive students. However, there are many very effective student management programs that should be included in college teacher training programs.

Far too many of our college professors don't seem to understand what is required to create better academic performance. They are often hung up on philosophical issues rather than those that are practical. The professors teach what they believe or have learned, which may not necessarily represent the most important elements of effective instruction. Until they focus on effective school research, they must bear part of the burden for our educational failures.

Every college teacher-training program should develop a formal course to help examine the schools that consistently produce the best school performance. They should place more emphasis on instructional strategies that help create successful performance. Teaching their students to use the best instructional materials will help improve the quality of new teachers.

The educational system needs to make sure students master skills that will help them be productive. Technical and vocational education should be made a priority.

Get the private sector involved in helping decide what skills are needed in the job market. I believe they would welcome the opportunity to help create qualified young people with marketable skills. Recent efforts to create more vocational programs have shown promise. For example, Arizona provides financial support for Joint Technical Education Districts that allow students to participate in college or vocational training while going to high school, and often receiving dual high school and college credit. These students clearly understand that a better future is achievable and that they must be successful if they're to continue participating in job training programs.

In the early 20th century, American education had far greater standards and expectations. The typical American high school had several different "tracks" they considered important to help meet the needs of their students. Without getting into the merits or problems with "tracking," I can tell you that 100 years ago high schools typically had several different programs that provided vocational, classical, and college-bound programs.

Unfortunately, many years ago in American history, vocational programs consisted only of females enrolled in some cooking and sewing classes. However, even those girls were required to demonstrate basic competencies in higher-level mathematics, English, writing, and foreign language that may have included either Latin or Greek. Most of the students were required to demonstrate advanced mathematics skills while today schools have to offer "basic" mathematics programs for incoming high school students because they can't even perform basic mathematic functions and are not prepared for algebra. Some of these programs are often referred to as "transitional" mathematics. Far too many students can't meet state writing standards and have real troubles reading.

These troubles start in elementary school!

If we are to continue to succeed as a nation, we must break the cycle and raise our standards. Students who are achieving should be provided with enriched instruction. Some of the best schools in our states and nation require an application and enrollment is not guaranteed. Parental involvement is mandatory and often supported by signed agreements or contracts. Those schools do not accept poor performance and take extraordinary measures to assure all of their students meet required expectations.

Some teachers in for-profit schools are paid according to their students' performances. Merit pay can work if our teachers are provided with an opportunity to understand and learn what it takes to help make sure their students perform appropriately. Professional growth is important, but must be provided by educators that have clearly demonstrated their own success in the classroom.

Our priorities for current educational funding should be reviewed. We must stop spending the greatest portion of our available school funds on students who will not be successful or, most importantly, do not care about school.

The philosophy that we can see the future through the eyes of the past is important. We must return to the days when American education was the best in the world. Examine what we did in those days and help develop a plan to change the current system. While it is a vastly different world today, the philosophical foundations that made education so good can be used to develop a new path for future educational programs. If we can do that and use the new technologies that weren't available even 20 years ago, we could climb out of mediocrity and create the very best educational system in the world. That will help our country continue to be the strongest and most powerful country in the world.

Chapter 8

ARE CHARTER SCHOOLS A GOOD ALTERNATIVE?

There are more than 560 charter schools in Arizona. These schools serve approximately 232,000 students and are adding more than 10,000 students every year. The average charter school receives approximately $2,730 less than the average public school. Charter schools usually receive a higher proportion from states and a lower portion from local sources.[37]

Nationally, 17 percent of charter school students performed significantly better than if they had attended their neighborhood public school. Research shows students in charter high schools score higher on college entrance exams and are more likely to graduate from high school and attend college than similar students in public schools.

The purpose of providing some current information regarding students' performance on tests is to help ensure that the first steps in choosing a school for your children is to carefully examine student performance at schools being considered.

Enrollment in a charter school may be a good alternative. Performance information is easily accessible on the Internet. Simply search for individual schools or district scores. Test scores are available for both charter and public schools. While the overall performance of charter school students may be a little better than public schools, parents should consider other factors in deciding which schools to choose for their children.

The "basic or traditional" schools in the Phoenix area are very popular among parents because they produce better student test scores. Public schools should provide more choices for their students and accept the fact that parents are more knowledgeable about which schools are the best.

Chapter 9

MAXIMIZING ENGAGED LEARNING

Engaged learning time is the time students are actively engaged in learning tasks. Students engaged during instruction will have more positive instructional outcomes. It is possible to measure and quantify engagement levels of the students. Students are not engaged when off-task, even though they are not creating any classroom disruption. Administrators can't give you an accurate picture of how much the students are engaged without visiting classrooms and trying to quantify student engagement rates. Engagement time is generally not considered in the evaluation of teachers, but it is possible to measure and quantify engagement levels of students. An excellent tool for administrators and teachers is the publication *How to Increase Learning Time*.[38] Teachers can use peer teachers to visit their classrooms and help measure the amount of instructional engagement.

Too much valuable instructional time is wasted in public elementary schools.

I believe that morning is the best time for teaching and learning. Time wasted in transition includes classroom changes from one instructional subject to another or movement to lunch and recess. It frustrates me to see recesses scheduled during the most optimal learning time in the morning. In visiting one elementary school in Texas, I noticed the first recess break was scheduled for 9:30 a.m. when school began at 8:15 a.m. The recess was scheduled for 15 minutes, but it took more than 25 minutes to get students to the playground and back to the classroom.

Some districts schedule half days for "teacher planning or training" activities. While teacher training is a good thing, I am not supportive of using student instruction time for teacher training.

I used engagement rate analysis in the evaluation of less effective teachers. It is especially important to help marginal or even poor teachers improve the amount of student engagement in their classrooms. I will never forget the principal's comment during my visit to a basic public school in Mesa, Arizona. He told me he regularly checks the school schedule to help ensure all teachers abide by exact schedules so that no instruction time is wasted. He discussed the fact that he could make less effective teachers successful if they administer the instructional program appropriately. I actually watched him use his watch to monitor dismissal times for lunch recess! Initially I thought this was overkill until I learned how important allocated instruction is in successful instructional programs. The achievement of the students at that school was one of the best in the state.

It is critical in measuring engaged learning to understand non-engaged time. Non-engaged time includes students that are off task for any reason. This could include transition time, socializing, dreaming (one of my own frailties as a young student), or working on something other than what instructional task is required. Some transition is necessary such as taking roll, changing instructional activities, sharpening pencils, or dealing with discipline issues to name a few.

A good alternative would be to require students to read during the classroom transition. The fundamental school required students to have a book to read when the teacher was dealing with non-instructional issues such as taking roll at the beginning of the day. When students finish an instructional activity before other students, they should pick up their book and read until all the children are finished. Reading during transition is important. I will deal with the issue of total allocated instruction and engaged learning later in this book.

In the fundamental program the engagement rate almost always exceeded 90 percent, a fact that is incredible. Even good schools rarely have more than 65 percent student engagement during the actual instructional day.

Working with upwards of 30 students a day is difficult. As a result, it is common for teachers to use strategies that allow themselves a little "mental break" time. I clearly understand the situation. I first taught high school students having five classes per day with up to four different subjects to teach. The problem is mental breaks are "time wasters." During my career I commonly saw elementary teachers assign a writing exercise and ask students to draw a picture with their writing. Often, the art portion of the activity took more time than the actual writing portion of the exercise. Teachers who minimize time wasters efficiently use allocated time to teach important skills that will improve student performance.

The quantity of time teaching is important. If every teacher could carefully manage classroom activities and improve the students engaged in learning by only fifteen minutes a day they would create an extra two weeks of instruction! Think about it! Eliminating transition or wasted time just fifteen minutes a day creates the equivalent of an extra two weeks of instruction!

It was always fun for me to see other educators try to figure out why the fundamental school students did so well. The most important thing we did besides changing the instructional program was to increase the total amount of instruction time.

In building the district program we looked at all of the elementary school schedules in the community. That information gave us excellent data to build the district and fundamental programs. We took the required time mandates of the state and compared it to the actual instruction time in the elementary schools in the community.

We were surprised to find some of the elementary schools were not even meeting the minimum time requirements required of the state. As a result, we created more instruction time in our daily school schedules. At that time the state required a minimum of 240 minutes of primary instruction daily or a total of 42,000 minutes during the 175 days of school for primary students in grades one through three. (The school calendars in most states have increased the number of days taught in to 180 days.) The district's primary school students had 345 minutes of school each day or 60,375 minutes of instruction for the school year. This was equivalent to 251 days of school during the year. The fundamental school students had even more daily instruction equivalent to 262 days of school. It should not have been a surprise that the fundamental school students did even better. If the fundamental students participated in the optional resource program, they had an equivalent school year of 306 days. I would estimate that more than 75 percent of the students participated in the before and after-school resource program. I don't think the other schools understood how the amount of time taught was such an important factor.

As a principal, it was common for me to hear teachers claim the whole week of school prior to Christmas or the end of the school year was a waste. "The students are just too excited to pay attention in school." Most schools have special events for holiday programs. They are really important to the children and parents. The parents of the fundamental school helped create holiday programs for the students that only occurred after school. In fact, the last day of the school year was a testing day for students. We made every effort to make sure students understood that instruction time was sacred and school is so important you can't waste any time.

We were even accused of child abuse because we had implemented an all-day kindergarten program, a first in the area. Today most school districts have some type of all-day kindergarten and there is talk of implementing preschool programs. I found children enjoyed learning and readily accepted the school schedule. This is especially true since the after-school holiday programs created for the students by parents were incredible!

Chapter 10

TECHNOLOGY AND EDUCATION

In my opinion there is a breaking point to the value of technology in American schools. It is disappointing to see two-year-olds transfixed to a smart phone in grocery carts at the grocery store. Texting friends in the same cafeteria at lunch borders on ridiculous. Most elementary schools do not allow cell phones for a good reason. While computers, the Internet, computer tablets, and teacher smart boards can provide incredibly valuable educational resources, they should never replace direct teacher instruction at the elementary school level.

Computers proved to be the main instructional delivery system for many children during the pandemic. Computer equipment and applications such as FaceTime and Zoom became important tools that could deliver instruction to the COVID-19 homebound students.

I have always been especially impressed with the Internet as a source of information. Teachers and students can find any information they need or want. It is important that they utilize this tremendous resource. The fundamental program was first established in 1981, well before technology became so important in American education. At that time, computers in schools and districts did not exist. However, cutting-edge technology was an important element in the fundamental school program.

The school had one of the first networked computer labs in the country. At the time, most basic conservative educators were wary of technology. But the computer labs in the fundamental school and district garnered significant attention and ultimately positive praise. The computer labs were not used for fun and games but instead were available to help augment instruction-based programming. The older children were even taught basic keyboarding skills. We were careful to consider the ages of students and fine motor skills of those in keyboarding activities. All the students cherished their time in the computer labs.

In the case of the fundamental school district their computer labs were "cutting edge" at the time. At that time computer equipment was very expensive and not readily available. However, one of the district's teachers was very computer literate and was able to network old Radio Shack TRS-80 computers, while providing as many as 24 computer stations in a laboratory by "daisy chaining" two server computers with other student computers. Those dinosaur machines were surprisingly cheap and, although the Radio Shack TRS-80 computers quickly became obsolete, the district's computer labs represented a huge leap for computer technology.

Many educators now consider technology an important fundamental element in instruction. It can be effective in helping with instruction and has become especially helpful in providing instruction to students with more severe physical disabilities.

The use of computers in education has grown exponentially as technology has improved. Schools today have incorporated more sophisticated technology in their programs. I am particularly impressed with "smart board" technology as it fits well with direct instruction efforts and clearly provides an effective use of technology. Schools can use computers and technology to enhance instruction and provide an efficient delivery system for students.

During the worst time in the pandemic, technology was the only option for instruction in many public schools. The doors of schools were most often closed. However, computers should never replace direct instruction from teachers in the classroom. Students continue to use desktop computers and computer tablets to help provide meaningful communication and instruction with schools. It is not surprising that large computer companies are encouraging the use of technology in the instructional process. As with any effort, the effective use of technology is directly dependent on the ability and training of teachers.

Chapter 11

TEST-WISENESS: HELPING TO IMPROVE A CHILD'S PERFORMANCE

Some schools have formal programs that help teach students how to take tests. Teaching students the strategies to use when taking a standardized test is a good practice. However, there is a lot of pressure on teachers for students to perform. In a few cases, teachers have crossed the line and either broken the general rules in administering the test or even helped students to answer questions. In most states, there are serious consequences for cheating on state testing programs. The consequences for breaking the rules may even include the loss of teacher certification. Nothing should ever be done to artificially inflate student performance.

However, I believe teaching students how to take tests is important. When you do so you are helping remove common variables that might negatively affect a student's performance. If students do not have basic information on how to take tests, their performances might not accurately represent their ability and knowledge.

Teachers must teach students how to manage their time during test-taking situations. Students need to learn how to mark their answers and use keys that might help them select the correct answers. Students also need to practice test-taking situations.

There are many private vendors available that specialize in helping prepare students for the SAT or ACT examinations. I will never forget my oldest daughter's first effort at taking the SAT as a senior in high school. She was an average student but a high achiever with excellent grades. She was very disappointed in her scores and asked me to help her prepare to take the test a second time.

Most high school students can take these tests more than once to improve their performance. I used several simple strategies as a result of her request for help. I purchased SAT preparation materials and had her practice taking sample tests using the same conditions and constraints required in the actual test-taking situations. She practiced time management and strategies to help her choose the correct answers during actual testing conditions. We talked about getting ready for the test. I gave her some simple recommendations like showing up for the test a few minutes early and taking extra pencils to use on the test. I remember her counselor telling me her performance would not improve by taking the test more than once. In the case of my own daughter, that was not true.

Knowing that my daughter was especially anxious when taking tests we planned all activities the day the test was scheduled. As an athlete, she ran a few fast miles early that morning to help relieve tensions and was ready to leave home well before testing began. As a result of her pretest efforts, her overall scores improved by about 300 points, a significant improvement.

The situation is the same for elementary children. Just choosing the answer on a scan-type answer sheet helps to create a new situation for which children might not be comfortable. Making sure you manage your time to answer questions or helping children become more confident are important variables that can positively influence test results. How can children be successful in test-taking situations if they are not familiar with the format of the test? Teaching a student how to use a scan-type answer sheet is important.

In the fundamental school, teachers practiced test-taking skills with the students. Sometimes, teachers used scan-type answer sheets and taught students strategies to help answer questions. Most importantly, they taught time management skills while taking a test.

As a student I clearly remember having to correct my answer sheet because I had not been taught to use a blank piece of paper to help me correctly choose the answer on the right-numbered row. I would not have needed to take extra time to erase and correct my errors if this had been explained to me.

Remember, test-wiseness helps remove variables and creates a more accurate summary of a student's ability and knowledge.

Chapter 12

CHARTER SCHOOLS

Charter schools have an advantage over public elementary schools. They can build unique programs without interference. They often offer alternatives not usually available in public schools, including more traditional instructional programs.

If you want to work in a charter school, you must be willing to accept the philosophy of the program. Reforming public school programs is difficult because of many barriers, some of which include uninformed school boards, administrators, and teachers. This is especially true of teacher organizations that can have a tremendously negative impact on the operation of schools. As an example, teachers often control the adoption of instruction materials even though they may not be as effective as other proven programs. The problem is one of ignorance. Many administrators and teachers just don't know what makes a good instructional program. If they were knowledgeable about effective research and used the information, their students' performance would improve. That is especially sad considering the information contained in effective school research is readily available to everyone!

I meet regularly for breakfast with some of my former colleagues and teachers. One morning, one of my high school teachers mentioned the fact that charter schools do well because they draw all the good students away from public schools. This may be true to a certain extent. Parents have become more educated, and it's a good thing they are concerned about the education their children receive. Choice is important and I believe public school elementary educators need to understand how important programming is to parents. There would be little need for charter schools if public schools offered alternatives and created more successful programs.

You can get a lot of information regarding charter schools on the Internet. I used data from the Arizona website as most of my experiences were in that state.[39] Critical information is available on the Internet in every state education department website in the nation.

The emergence of the charter school movement in Arizona in the 90s might be a valid indicator of parent dissatisfaction with public school programs. What happened in Arizona also happened in other states. Charter schools offer programming choice and sometimes tout programs not normally available in public schools. Most importantly, charter schools are able to build new programs without the need to change or revise existing programs.

Currently, there are more than 3.2 million charter school students in the United States. Other parents are opting to place their children in parochial schools. Parochial schools serve students whose parents are willing to pay tuition to receive an education for their children even though their enrollment may transcend a religious education. It is no wonder school districts are creating sophisticated advertising programs in hopes of attracting more students.

Since school enrollment numbers are tied directly to state funding on a per pupil basis, public schools lose funding if they lose students to charter schools!

School legislation in Arizona was passed in 1994, allowing the development of charter school programs. In that year public charter students in the state outperformed the statewide average pass rate by 9 percentage points on the English language arts test. In addition, charter school students in the state outperformed the statewide average pass rate by 8 percentage points on the mathematics test. Of all grade levels and subject areas within public charter schools, third-grade math students achieved the greatest gains over four years, increasing pass rates by 14 percentage points from 47 percent to 61 percent on the 2015 to 2018 state-mandated examinations. In addition, 29 of the top 50 schools on the state math test are charter schools. Public charter students in all racial and ethnic groups outperformed the statewide pass rate for their peer groups. Charter schools also outperformed public school students in all subjects tested at all grade levels.[40]

Chapter 13

FINDING MORE INFORMATION AND THE BEST SCHOOLS

The Arizona Department of Education ranks all its 1,029 elementary schools. You can use state department information in every state and get details about your district or school. The rankings are calculated based on the state-mandated test scores in mathematics, language arts, and science. Parents can use rank information to help understand the quality of any elementary school program anywhere in the state and nation. A school's rank in comparison to all the other schools in the state is a very important statistic and should render serious consideration by parents, whether school districts like it or not.

The following chart contains information based on recent test information provided by the Arizona Department of Education (ADE). Additional information for the rankings is provided by the National Center for Education Statistics (NCES) and the US Department of Education.[41]

CHARTER SCHOOLS RANKED IN THE TOP 30 SCHOOLS IN ARIZONA

Name of School	Arizona Rank
BASIS (Scottsdale)	3
BASIS (Chandler)	4
Chandler Basic School	5
BASIS (Oro Valley)	7
BASIS (Chandler Primary)	11
BASIS (Peoria)	13
Mexicayota Academy	19
Scottsdale Country School	20
BASIS (Tucson Primary)	23
Adams Traditional Academy	24
Bright Beginnings School	25
Great Hearts Academy (Scottsdale)	28

In Arizona, 12 of the top 30 schools are charter schools. By any standard that is phenomenal!

PUBLIC SCHOOL ELEMENTARY SCHOOL PROGRAMS IN THE TOP 30 SCHOOLS IN ARIZONA

Name of School	Arizona Rank
Mesa Academy for Advances Studies	1
Knox Gifted Academy	2
Neely Traditional School	6
Franklin at Brimhall Elementary	9
Vista del Sur Accelerated	10
Chandler Traditional Academy	12
Chandler Traditional School	15

Montessori Schoolhouse	16
Cheyenne Traditional School	26

Several school districts in the metropolitan Phoenix area have established what they term basic or traditional schools, all of which have excellent test scores. All of them are very popular with parents. Basic or traditional school programs are among the top 30 schools in Arizona. Most of these district schools allow parents living outside attendance boundaries to participate in their programs.

School districts that offer more choices and provide special academic programs are generally more successful in producing better student achievement. Higher student performance correlates positively with parent satisfaction. Some Arizona districts seem to have figured out what is needed to help attract students. Many of those schools provide special programs for more advanced students.

The fundamental school magnet program discussed provided an option that is now available in other charter schools. Parents of the fundamental school had a choice and were involved in the development of the program. Their support and encouragement were key elements in the tremendous success of the program. The school's achievement test scores were among the best in the state of Arizona in all subjects tested.

There is no way to predict what would have happened if the charter school legislation did not pass in Arizona in 1994. If public schools provided special or alternative school choice it would likely have eliminated the need for charter school programs.

Interest in the fundamental school continued to be tremendous until the school's philosophy waned over the years with new administrations and school board members. When the administration and governing board eliminated the fundamental school program there was an outcry from the parents.

There are now at least seven charter schools in the community discussed, serving almost 3,000 students. Since the fundamental school program was eliminated, several new schools have been built, including a new Catholic high school. Charter school enrollment continues to grow. Since schools are funded based on enrollment. Losing student enrollment has a negative effect on the amount of fiscal support available to public schools. Loss of enrollment is very difficult for all schools and districts. If schools and districts were offering successful programs that parents want, there would be no need for advertising expenditures.

It is important to list the ranking information for schools in the current fundamental school community. Look at the movement in rankings in your state from year to year. Improved rankings are realistically the result of efforts to help improve programming. The following chart provides rankings for all the schools in the fundamental school community.

CURRENT SCHOOLS IN THE FORMER FUNDAMENTAL SCHOOL COMMUNITY COMPARED TO THE RANK OF ALL THE OTHER 1029 ARIZONA SCHOOLS

(Arizona Department of Education 2019)

School	District Rank in State	Rank Loss/Gain
STEM Program	96	-14
School A	383	-56
School B	504	+7
School C	506	-96
School D	519	+59
School E	520	+36
School F	531	-155
School G	535	+4
School H	560	-20
School I	562	-77
School J	581	-123
School K	611	+143
School L	642	+229
School M	654	-79
School N	655	-90
School O	663	-119
School P	665	-262
Former Fundamental School	709	-112
School Q	728	-91
School R	728	+95

School S	734	+81
School T	841	-56
School U	842	+98
School V	850	+132
School X	868	+180
School Y	919	-19

The few schools showing the best rank improvement will be discussed in more detail. In looking at the information, you will notice the trend in the community's schools was to lose ranking status even before the pandemic. Over half the schools in the former fundamental school district lost rank status. The former fundamental school lost 112 rank positions in comparison to other schools in the state.

What is going on?

Parents should understand the statistical information provided by looking at school ranking information. Minor movement in the rankings may be influenced by variables that affect testing information, such as student mobility, numbers of limited or non-English speaking students, and the number of non-certified teaching staff, to name a few factors. However, I would consider school ranking information very important because it is a critical indicator of academic success and helps to provide a comparative analysis with all the other schools in the community and state. The school rank information includes all the 1029 Arizona elementary schools, and parents should be very concerned about any major loss in those rankings.

I was interested in the movement of district schools in the ranking process. School board members should expect to see positive improvements in school ranks. One elementary school located in the most impoverished area in the community with many minority students improved its ranking 132 positions. That is impressive.

Sometimes coming from behind creates pride. As a competitive distance runner, I often started at the back of the group of race participants just to see how many runners I could pass. Almost all the schools in the community I have discussed lost ranking status, with some moving significantly in the wrong direction. Are school board members even aware of ranking information or do they even care about ranking status?

Only a few of the area's schools achieved a significantly higher school ranking as compared to the rest of Arizona's schools. One of its schools improved an impressive 229 rank positions of the total 1,029 elementary schools in the state, an impressive improvement of 22 percent. The school's principal is a personal friend and was formally one of my administrative hires. She is a very competent administrator with very impressive credentials, including experience in special education, federal projects, school publicity and, most important, curriculum and instruction. If I were interested in school improvement, I would look to the schools that create the most improvement in ranking and would certainly make it a point to examine what they are doing to help create positive improvement.

Chapter 14

VOUCHERS

One of the greatest concerns of public school educators is the potential use of school vouchers to fund and allow parents to send their children to any school they desire. Vouchers are important because they will pressure schools to improve and provide programs that garner the best student performance. I believe a voucher school program is important. I am sure many public-school employees would be surprised by my position since my entire career was as a public-school educator.

Tax-paying parents deserve school choice and deserve the ability to send their children to the best schools!

In reviewing the top quarter of the school ranking results, everyone should note that most of Arizona's best schools are either charter schools or district magnet schools that provide traditional-type programs.

Chapter 15

GADSDEN ELEMENTARY SCHOOL DISTRICT – SAN LUIS, ARIZONA

The Arizona Department of Education provides school ratings each year utilizing a simple grading system from A to F. All but one of the elementary schools in the Gadsden Elementary School District received a rating of A by the Arizona Department of Education. What is the district doing to meet educational challenges? The district is located in San Luis, Arizona, on the border with Mexico. The district is the only one I have referenced specifically by name with their permission in *The Longest Pandemic*.

School ratings are based primarily on academic achievement and progress using multiple data points. The ratings assigned to all school districts are data-driven and published annually for every school in the country as well as Arizona.

The academic growth of the students in the Gadsden Elementary School District shows how a school district can make academic improvements. The district has addressed many challenges, the most significant being the district's student demographic makeup. In this district, 100 percent of the students are Hispanic, 91 percent of which come from low-income families. Almost half of the district's students are learning English for the first time, which is another significantly challenging situation. The student-teacher ratio is larger than the average in the state, and per pupil expenditures are $1,650 less than the state average.

I met with the administration to find out what the district is doing to achieve such positive academic growth. I was surprised to learn that they were less concerned with the school state grade ratings and more concerned with their ranking among schools in the county and state, a better indication of their focus on achieving the best possible school performance.

I would not be surprised to see their schools continue to improve. It was clear to me in the interview that the administration was proud of their schools and cared deeply about student performance. All but one of the elementary schools in the Gadsden Elementary School District improved their school rankings in 2019. Most of the schools' rankings improved by more than 100 spots in the state's 1,029 schools, with one school improving its ranking position by 229 positions. Given the number of elementary schools in the state, that figure is very impressive. While the Gadsden School District had significant ranking results, almost all of the other public schools in the area lost comparative ranking status!

School ratings and rankings are readily available on the Internet and are very important to schools, since more open registration options are available to parents. Parents can access this information on state school education websites or even SchoolDigger.com.

There are numerous examples of programming excellence. The district places an emphasis on helping to improve the culture of its students, schools, and community. Having had a music background myself, I was particularly impressed with the district's commitment to a formal music education program, including a band program for all its elementary students. Every school has a music program that includes instrumental music. The elementary school students are provided with musical instruments and a certified music teacher. As a former musician, I believe participation in a music program often correlates with positive student achievement, school climate, and an optimal learning environment. The district's band has gained a national reputation for quality and has resulted in significant community pride.

The administration and teachers at every school in the district carefully assess the academic performance of students and establish specific individual achievement goals. The district's teachers use authentic assessment, which requires all students to demonstrate specific skills and competencies. The district has partnered with Arizona State University and the National Institute for Excellence in Teaching to help develop a Teacher Advancement Program (TAP) that provides a specific system for teachers to grow professionally within the school and district. The TAP Program requires school leaders and teachers to reflect on best practices and continuously strive to become more effective.

Due to the support provided by the principal, master and mentor teachers, the observation process, and participation in weekly cluster meetings, everyone is working toward common goals for the students. They continuously work to improve the quality of instruction. The TAP philosophy is important and allows teachers to pursue upward mobility. They strive to become better teachers, mentor other teaching peers, and lastly become master teachers.

Master teachers are assigned to each school and provide extensive classroom observations, coaching, and data analysis that I believe is the key to the excellence of their program. The master teachers spend most of their time in the classroom and directly interact with both the students and teachers.

The district provides opportunities for job embedded professional development and supports instructionally focused accountability. The master teachers are knowledgeable in content areas and meet regularly with individual teachers and, if necessary, students. Interactions are normally positive with the emphasis on teacher and student performance.

My greatest frustration as a principal was the inability to get into the classrooms. Paperwork and other duties prevent the ability of a principal to visit classrooms, which is the most important responsibility of a principal. Continuous classroom observations and staff development with coaching follow-up are critical components necessary to create effective instruction. The Gadsden Elementary School District has developed a procedure to help improve instruction, and it has certainly paid off!

One of the biggest potential instructional time-wasters can be when substitute teachers are needed. Providing a substitute teacher when the regular teacher is absent is a necessity, and every school will have to do it on occasion. The critical need for substitute teachers is tremendous.

Arizona requires anyone wishing to substitute to have a college degree and a valid fingerprint card. However, it also provides a method for individual districts to acquire emergency substitutes. Applicants must have a high school diploma, general education diploma from high school, proof of high school graduation, or an associate degree. They must also have received a recommendation from the school district.

Most of the instruction during a teacher's absence is never as good as the regular teacher and sometimes it's worthless. Substitute teachers are normally required to use instructional plans created by the regular classroom teachers. Often these plans utilize more "busy work" activities that are also often of questionable instructional value.

I recently volunteered to help the Gadsden Elementary School District by acting as a non-paid substitute teacher. I really wanted to see how the non-English speaking Hispanic children were doing in the district and help the district increase its substitute pool without increasing their costs. I was also interested in finding out what the district is doing to create such excellent student performance.

To my amazement, I was told I'd have to complete the substitute training before I could work as a substitute teacher. My pride was bruised, and I wondered why I couldn't qualify as a substitute when I already had six administrative or teaching certificates and other endorsements. Further, I had experience at every grade level in my career. I have evaluated teachers at every grade and had a background that would surely make me a good substitute teacher.

After thinking about the situation, I decided to "bite the bullet" and attend their three-day substitute-training program. I wanted to find out what they could teach me that I didn't already know. Surprisingly, their training was one of the most professionally gratifying programs I have ever attended. They provided information relative to every school and instructional methods consistent with their district and likely not even available in formal teacher training programs.

During the training, they provided the approximately 30 "trainees" with methods to help children with vocabulary and work in their interactive notebooks and K-1 journals. They discussed special education program needs and how to read to students, how they expect teachers to summarize instructional reading materials, and provided specific strategies for reading, writing, math, and science instruction. They also provided valuable information to use Google Suite and the students' computer tablets. Most importantly, they provided detailed information on the required student management program and effective methods to assure the students remain on task during the teacher's absence. The district's expectations were clear in that they want their substitute teachers to be effective.

I inquired as to the backgrounds of the people attending the workshop. Most of the "trainees" were currently students in college. While none of the participants had four-year college degrees, many were enrolled in teacher education programs. It was clear to me that the district wants to "grow their own teachers" and make sure the students have effective instruction whenever the regular teacher is absent. The trainees are required to shadow existing teachers for several days before being paid, providing additional practical experience. This solidified my opinion that the district is serious about implementing effective instructional methods.

Arizona has established an incentive program to recognize outstanding educational programs. Additional school funds are provided to schools through the State's Results-Based Funding Program.[42] Awards are based on academic progress measured by Arizona's testing program. Each school's extra funding is dependent on how high they rank as compared to the other schools in the state using data from the mandated testing program. The amount of extra funding is based on a per pupil award of $440 per student. Eighty percent of each school's extra funding goes directly to teachers with the remaining 20 percent going to fund the instructional program. Three of the district's schools received a total of $546,951 in additional funding, most of which went directly to the staff in pay.

The Results-Based Funding Program's merit pay program works! Imagine how important the teachers feel about effective instruction. I am sure they want all of their teaching colleagues to perform to the best of their ability! Unfortunately, many teachers and especially teacher unions in America do not support merit pay programs. This district is a perfect example of how merit pay systems can help improve American education!

Chapter 16

BASIS CHARTER SCHOOLS

BASIS Charter Schools occupied five of the top 15 school programs in all the 1,029 elementary schools in Arizona.[43] According to their website "We have studied the principles and practices of the best-performing schools in the world. We continue to consider what works well and analyze how to make the BASIS Charter School Curriculum better, year after year."[44]

This statement supports the entire concept of what I have been trying to convey. Look to proven success and use those strategies to improve your school or district. If public schools are ever to be more successful they must assume a competitive philosophy and learn what strategies lead to excellence.

Why are BASIS Charter Schools so successful?

1. Their administrators manage the curriculum as well as the scope and sequence of instruction.
2. Their teachers are masters in their content area.
3. Administrators or master teachers work directly in the classroom with teachers and students.
4. Students are required to master content an average of one grade level ahead of peers in all subjects.

5. Their instruction utilizes critical thinking skills. BASIS Charter School programs are expanding at a rapid rate. Their existence has created tremendous interest and will have a tremendously positive impact on the current school programs in any area they are located!

Chapter 17

SCHOOL DISTRICT WEBSITES

The current school district with the debunked fundamental school has a very nice website. If I were a parent looking to locate in a community and looked at the district's website, I might be impressed (not considering the student performance).

It is important that parents be cautious of school district website information. As an example, the district's website states that their average math and reading proficiency scores exceed the state average. The truth is that they exceed the state's average by only 1 percent, probably a result of the district's STEM school performance. In reality, the district's test scores are worse than 57 percent of the schools in the state. The fact that only one of 13 schools is doing well does not mean the district is excelling.

In reality, math and reading proficiency has dropped since 2014 and does not even come close to the achievement test scores of the original fundamental school. The district's website claims their achievement scores rank within the top 50 percent of the other 621 districts in Arizona (based on combined math and reading proficiency data for the 2016-2017 school year), a fact that is not impressive. Most of the district's school rankings dropped, some of which lost more than 100 ranking positions compared to other schools.

While some general information is important, parents should be wary of individual school website information. More specific information is available on state websites or other data contained on the Internet.

Chapter 18

THE NEGATIVE EFFECTS OF THE CORONAVIRUS PANDEMIC

Students in America have lost more than just academics. They suffered emotionally as a result of the pandemic. There is little doubt that the pandemic has had a tremendously adverse effect on American education and especially elementary school education. Recent test scores indicate the performance of American students continues to decline.

Information about the pandemic continues to be a source of controversy. Must everyone be forced to vaccinate even though they may have strong antibody protection from past virus sickness? Should everyone continue to wear masks even though the effectiveness of masks has been questioned? Are current vaccines effective? Is subsequent illness a possibility for those who have been vaccinated? Will new virus strains create more problems? Do current vaccinations for children have any long-term effects? How many additional vaccines will be needed?

My own view is that students should continue to attend school and their absence from school during the pandemic may have been worse than the negative effects of the virus. Parents should continue to make personal decisions based on available scientific data and their own beliefs. Mandating the vaccine seems to me an assault on personal freedoms, although I understand the argument from both sides of the issue. It is certainly frustrating to see really good students denied an education because they could not go to school or refused to wear masks, especially considering the questionable effectiveness of masks.

I feel that future student performance will likely show a further decline and if school performance doesn't slip, I would be even more concerned with the current quality of elementary education.

There has been a huge difference among school districts in response to the pandemic, as public information has been confusing. The different strategies schools have used to deal with the problem have also been confusing. Some canceled school altogether, some created distance learning strategies, and some created "hybrid" schedules.

The effort to provide distance-learning strategies for instruction may not have been generally successful, especially for students who do not have access to the Internet. Yet many larger school districts chose the distance-learning strategy in an effort to deal with the pandemic, including Los Angeles, Atlanta, Columbus, and Houston.

It is possible that distance learning has failed children and worsened achievement gaps by race and income. Access to computers and the internet in distance learning efforts has exacerbated poor performance, and many districts are not able to provide computer equipment for their students, and even if they could provide the equipment, the lack of Internet service remains a problem.

After a couple of weeks of no school, my youngest grandchild's school finally decided to do something for their students after the first virus outbreak. He was lucky to have his own computer tablet. When a distance-learning program was implemented the time he spent in interactions with his teacher was limited to only about 45 minutes each day while his school was closed.

Some schools delayed starts or reduced direct teacher-student interactions by staggering days of attendance or by reducing days taught. Many parents took the need for home instruction seriously while others were unable to address the need for home study, which will most certainly factor into future performance. I am concerned that proper instruction was not appropriately addressed, even in cases where parents did their best to provide home study.

Late in October of 2020, I was visited by a group of out-of-state hunters at my Wyoming home. During that two-week period, their children continued with an online school using my Internet service. I was pleasantly surprised at what I observed during their visit.

Makellah and Devlyn are students in the Long Beach Unified School District. Makellah attends a middle school, while her older brother Devlyn, was a freshman in high school, also in Long Beach. Both students were online the entire day Monday through Friday during their visit.

Makellah's online studies included mathematics, English, Spanish, science, and physical education. Devlyn's school day was equally long. His schedule included graphic design, English, Spanish, geometry, and history.

In speaking to the students about the situation, they seemed most concerned with the age of their computers. When I asked what happened to students without Internet service, they told me the district distributed "hot spots" to their students so that more students had access to Internet services.

Makellah and Devlyn are both very good students who, despite the difficulty with computer instruction and the fact that they missed their friends, seemed happy they could continue their studies. Their work was graded online and was based on the completion of school assignments. All their classes continued to be taught by professionally certified teachers.

Despite the difficult situation, I was impressed with the district's distance learning program. The students were engaged in the learning process and spent most of every school day working online with their peers and teachers. However, the students made it clear to me that the lack of direct interactions with their teachers and peers was devastating. They missed their classmates and were clearly not happy, which makes me even more suspicious of the psychological pressures resulting from isolation.

Unfortunately, I believe some teachers took advantage of the situation during the worst of the pandemic. But I believe most teachers wanted to work and missed their students.

Some teacher unions publicly stated they would financially support any of their teachers who refuse to return to school until the pandemic was eliminated. They issued conditions they believed necessary to open schools, even though all teachers were given priority vaccinations. The whole issue became personal. Many people have chosen not to participate in the vaccine program. They may have religious issues or feel strongly about vaccinations, especially a fast-tracked vaccination program. Yet now our students are faced with the consequences of time they lost while not in school.

According to many news outlets, the Chicago Public School teachers refused to return to the classroom. It is clear that the majority of teachers do not support more conservative issues and in particular, the need to open schools. The Chicago Teachers Union threatened a work stoppage over its school opening plan.

Almost universally, teacher associations and unions argued that schools need more money to operate. More money might help but it will not solve the problem. While I agree that additional resources may be needed, money is not the ultimate solution to school excellence.

News media outlets reported many demands of teachers. The United Teachers of Los Angeles made demands that have nothing to do with safety issues. They wanted to eliminate new charter school proposals. Other demands included things, such as Medicare for all, wealth taxes, and federal bailouts. Some of the teacher unions tried to use the pandemic to support the elimination of charter schools, voucher programs, the removal of police from schools, and, you guessed it, the elimination of standardized testing (the one element that can be used to evaluate school performance)!

Scientific information seems to indicate children can be safe in classrooms and that students are less susceptible to COVID-19. The negative effects of virus variants seem less pronounced than the original COVID-19. As a result, keeping children from attending school may have been a mistake. Yet, many parochial schools continued to serve students and, to the best of my knowledge, had few problems. They were required to wear masks and practice social distancing.

It seems we continue to get confusing information from government and media sources. The whole situation is frustrating for parents who have to make decisions about sending their children to schools.

How has the virus and boosters affected children? Will we ever know how many boosters will be needed? How quick and easy is it to get those "free" testing kits? Why does the supply chain problem always seem such a problem?

I believe that all Americans have the right to decide whether or not they participate in vaccination programs. My entire family was vaccinated, including my son-in-law, who is a pediatrician. My wife, a registered nurse, and I both chose vaccination and had the two booster shots. We were also given our booster shots because we both have secondary risk factors. Despite our vaccinations, we both eventually contracted the virus. My question is why? At one time I was under the impression that the vaccination programs would protect people from contracting the virus.

Recent information seems to indicate we will continue to need additional boosters, especially since we are at high risk. Regardless of how one feels about vaccination programs, the majority of serious infections are more prevalent in those who were not vaccinated. Yet some people who have been vaccinated and boosted twice continue to get sick. That has not been helpful to parents who are trying to decide what course of action to take, especially since a new vaccine is now available for very young children. The bad situation has seemingly become worse!

Student Resource Officers (SRO)

I was fortunate to have Student Resource Officers (SROs) assigned in many of the schools I served in my career. They are valuable assets that help schools deal with a multitude of issues. They are especially helpful with extracurricular programs. They provide aid for parents and work closely with counselors and teachers to deal with student and parent issues, including behavior.

In my opinion, the Student Resource Officer programs represent the perfect strategy that helps enhance a community policing effort, something I have continuously heard during the "defund the police" effort. It is simply stupid to think we can have safer schools and a safer nation by downsizing law enforcement. We must teach children the importance of law enforcement institutions and that they exist to help and not hurt. I believe all schools should have an SRO for many reasons, especially for school safety.

The latest elementary school shootings and the number of other mass shootings in the country are evil and senseless. It is doubtful that law enforcement or schools will ever be able to eliminate such absolutely heinous events. Ultimately, schools have the primary responsibility to keep students safe and should move forward to help deal with the possibility of future horrific events.

This will require expenditures beyond the capabilities of most districts and schools.

Our politicians must provide help to ensure the safety of American schools. There are resources but the waste of federal money is well documented. Would it be possible to reallocate some of the money sent to other countries around the world? At the risk of being labeled an "isolationist," we should take care of our own country before we can help every other country in the world.

The federal government should provide funding for Student Resource Officers for all schools in the country. In addition to security, SRO's can provide many other forms of assistance to schools. Their job descriptions should include additional elements beyond regular law enforcement requirements. They should possess a special empathy for children and help with extracurricular activities. SROs might be able to help counselors work with students and support stronger student management programs. They can make home visits and provide a level of safety that schools aren't able to provide.

There are also many infrastructure changes that schools will need to help make schools safe. The exterior of all schools should have more secure fences, specially designed to keep children on school grounds and intruders off. The fences should provide only one entrance, and the exit gate should be locked. Better windows are needed and security cameras should be installed throughout each campus. Video security systems are not expensive and all schools should move to install as many cameras as quickly as possible. Schools need only one access point and it should always be monitored. School

The Negative Effects of the Coronavirus Pandemic

personnel should be available at each entrance and exit location when the gates are unlocked.

I made it a practice to be at the entrance of my school every day to welcome students and encourage them to work hard. They seemed to love my presence.

School district personnel and SROs should have the ability to continually monitor students and visitors when entering the school. Non-school visitors should be channeled through the office and screened by office personnel. Visitors on campus should be given a nametag indicating they have been screened and approved to visit the school. An approved list of student visitors should be established and used in the office during the screening process. There should be no access to the school without screening in the office. Concerns from the office about any visitor should be communicated immediately to the administration and SRO with effective communication equipment.

The situation with shootings in our country may require drastic measures. Effective action by law enforcement will save many lives. Most have studied active shooting situations and most worked hard to respond more effectively when necessary.

Every student should be taught that they are part of a solution to the problem of violence. We should make sure students realize how important it is to be aware of warning signs. Concerns should be reported, and student and community cooperation will help address potential problems.

Already a common practice, lockdown procedures should be practiced regularly and taken seriously. I've had many actual and serious lockdowns in my career, the last being a lockdown at a large K-8 school because of a hostage situation in the neighborhood. We kept all of the students locked in school for five hours beyond dismissal and even served dinners until law enforcement allowed the students to leave campus. I spent those hours outside talking with parents and assuring them the students were safe. They were all very cooperative and sincerely appreciated the communication.

Chapter 19

CLASSROOM ORGANIZATION IN THE PANDEMIC

During the pandemic many schools began to focus more on furniture arrangement to achieve "social distancing" efforts. Schools are now reviving the use of individual desks and more traditional desk arrangements. A more traditional arrangement of student desks in elementary schools should never have been de-emphasized. Furniture arrangement in classrooms has an important impact on student engagement and learning.

I am amazed at the multitude of furniture arrangements one sees in elementary school classrooms. Non-traditional furniture arrangements do not meet most social distancing efforts and it seems as if every teacher has their own unique way to organize classrooms. In one undergraduate class I taught, I discussed classroom furniture arrangement as an important factor helping to keep students engaged and on task. My interactions with both undergraduate and graduate college education students convinced me that most teachers do not understand the importance of simple furniture arrangement in establishing an efficiently organized classroom.

When we first developed the fundamental school, we required more traditional classroom arrangements. In traditional classrooms, all the individual student desks are arranged in staggered rows and face the teacher at the front of the room. This arrangement is more effective in combination with direct instruction, with the teacher controlling the instruction. This is especially important when teachers use media equipment such as "smart boards" or other media in their instruction.

Traditional desk arrangements help create optimal visual contact with all of the students and are especially useful with larger classes. Tables can be situated around the edge of the rows of desks for small group work. Individual student desks are conducive to social distancing. Many schools and districts are scrambling to acquire individual student desks.

Although now obsolete, overhead projectors were particularly important in the fundamental school because of the school's use of direct instructional strategies in subjects, such as mathematics and writing. The use of computers and now "smart boards" are valuable for all subjects. Instruction in basic, traditional, or fundamental schools is always teacher-centered.

Perhaps my worst classroom experience came many years after I retired. I felt it important to understand what was happening in schools since I retired. I agreed to substitute teach in schools that could not provide adequate substitute staff. One of my assignments was as a primary teacher in a small elementary school. When I opened the classroom door I anticipated a challenge when I saw how the teacher had organized the classroom. Individual desks were pushed together and tables were placed sporadically throughout the classroom. That teacher had absolutely no idea how to organize a classroom. His obvious lack of appropriate classroom management resulted in a very bad substitute experience. That school day may have been the most miserable and longest in my entire career. That teacher needed a great deal of help.

Visitors to the fundamental school were amazed that we also used individual student ceramic eraser boards. In one instance, the teacher asked students to complete a mathematics problem. The students did so with their individual boards and held them up when they completed the problem. Regardless of how traditional this method was 100 years ago, the teacher was able to immediately understand the level of mastery of the students. Wow, this was a huge subject of conversation among visitors to the fundamental school!

A recent article in the local newspaper on the pandemic's impact on education addressed the potential negative impact on student performance. Like many district office administrators, an attempt was made to help minimize the impact of potential poor student achievement. Although without having data, one district office administrator claimed assessments in English language arts and math revealed incremental growth in those subjects as students took the assessments at home in a remote learning environment rather than in a classroom setting.

I wonder about the validity of home instruction. Without data, one district office administrator claimed students did not lose a whole year of learning. One of the teachers interviewed asked the reporter not to advertise student scores. Another parent claimed that home study had been good for their child. This seems a rare feeling among parents. I know that parents and older siblings have tried to help, but missing direct instruction from a teacher is critical.

It looks like American students should have returned to school much earlier, or better yet, should have remained in school!

Chapter 20
TEACHER UNIONS AND THEIR EFFECT ON SCHOOLS

In general, charter schools have been more successful than public schools, considering student achievement. Charter schools have the opportunity to develop programs without interference from union policies. They often develop their own programs based on educational research and what works best.

Governing boards have a difficult time dealing with the "happiness" politics of teachers, and since school board members are normally politically elected officials, they may quickly concede to the wishes of teachers and employees.

As a school superintendent, I was subject to scrutiny from some teachers who did not agree with the effective school strategies I knew would improve instruction. Teachers tried to make life miserable for our administrators during one particular school board election. Some teachers actively supported the election of new school board members they believed would be more supportive of their philosophies. They were not successful in their efforts to change the school board in the election as their candidates endured a huge voter loss. However, before the final public vote was made, someone put more than a dozen signs in my front yard supporting some of the school board candidates they wanted. That night, someone defecated on my front porch. Even more sadly, someone poisoned our dog, a cherished pet we considered a member of our family. Those situations can be ugly and stressful. The fact is that some administrators and school board members avoid difficult decisions in order to "keep everyone happy." Charter schools generally do not have to deal with these kinds of problems.

In recent years, unions and even teacher associations in "right to work" non-union states have become much more aggressive in exerting their influence on many national issues that may have nothing to do with education. Some teacher unions have taken active stances on abortion rights and the "criminalization of border crossings" by illegal aliens. Some opposed the construction of the border wall and have become increasingly active in salary and benefit issues. They want to eliminate charter schools and school vouchers and will intensely fight any merit pay system. They will fight to eliminate any instructional program they do not endorse, which is the worst possible situation in establishing instructional excellence.

If that worries you, think about The American Federation of Teachers (AFT), one of the largest unions in the country. The American Federation of Teachers website clearly supports the following:[45]

Oppose many credible education reforms aimed at fixing our failing schools.

Want to "reimagine" education and have more influence on future programs.

Influence conditions to reopen schools.

Encourages liberal activism by supporting such organizations as Black Lives Matter.

Promote tenure and protect teachers regardless of their competence.

Control course content and instructional materials to be used in educational programs.

Represent the interests of teachers regardless of their abilities.

Rich Lowry, editor of the *National Review*, referencing teachers and the pandemic, puts it clearly, "They've fought for teachers to get paid for not working and they've placed children's well-being and education low on their list of priorities."[46]

Not surprisingly, the AFT opposes performance-based pay and would be happy to eliminate charter schools, vouchers, and tests to evaluate performance. They oppose the ability to terminate incompetent teachers and extra pay for hard-to-recruit teachers with special qualifications. Yet they want to extend collective bargaining ability.

If you live in a state where teacher unions are particularly active, you need to pay even more attention to existing school programs!

Chapter 21

CRITICAL RACE THEORY (CRT)

The Critical Race Theory (CRT) has become a major topic of conversation, perhaps stimulated by several "protest" incidents in America, particularly after the George Floyd situation. One definition of CRT is a way of thinking about America's history through the lens of racism. Somehow people who subscribe to the philosophy think that racism is systemic in our country. Recently I have even heard that all members of the Republican Party are extremists or racist. Can that really be true?

Subscribers to CRT believe that race is culturally invented and not biological. Its philosophic foundation appears to stem from the days of forced labor and slavery in America or our historically poor treatment of indigenous Native Americans.

We have come a long way in America and, I believe, have accomplished many things to help our country address racial inequality. It is certainly true we can continue to make improvements. However, many CRT believers support the rewriting of American history and persuade white people that they are inherently racist.

Their efforts to spread these ideas will certainly become a more serious matter of discussion.

The argument for including CRT concepts in what to teach our children, particularly at the elementary level, is just plain nuts for many reasons!

The Idea of "Reimagining" for Elementary Education in America

I am hopeful that things will get back to normal in 2023. We must get the students back in school and build more effective programs of instruction.

In the initial days of President Biden's tenure, I listened to the need for "reprograming or reimagining" our American culture. The whole idea of equity training seems entirely bogus to me, especially if we are trying to build a more unified America. The idea of retraining or reprogramming many of America's elementary teachers really is justified but not to include "equity" training. They must take steps to understand what is effective, incorporating those strategies into their instructional programs.

Until such steps are taken to help improve teaching quality and the amount of time students are taught, American parents will continue to see further declines in the quality of elementary school programs.

The need to change our instructional programs to include critical race theory is just plain crazy. The fact that I do not believe in the philosophy of this effort and that I believe it will create a less unified nation is not the point. Schools must focus on building a more effective instructional foundation. Besides being something

I feel inappropriate, there is simply not enough instructional time available to introduce a subject of this nature, especially when our students are not performing at even average levels. This is especially true in the primary elementary school grades. It is my hope and observation that parents continue to fight against the inclusion of CRT in their schools. Demand to see how teachers are using available instruction time.

I think some educators and particularly school counselors have tried to disguise CRT philosophies. "Social and Emotional Learning (SEL)" is a brainchild instructional program of the Wallace Foundation, an organization dedicated to "Foster equity and enrich young students."[47] I have read media reports on the supposed effectiveness of these types of programs. I believe CRT labels are often avoided in media reports. I have recently seen elementary counselors claim teachers already have so much on their plate that they need to help teach. I also read where one SEL counselor works with small groups of students as early as second grade "to prepare students for middle school." I would rather see more instruction time in the basic subjects of reading, math, and language arts.

Most of these programs were likely not have been approved by school boards or parents. You can't tell me the Social and Emotional Learning effort doesn't resemble CRT in nature, especially since it emphasizes the teaching of "desired traits." I noticed one classroom bulletin board stressing the important message of "courage."

C (Care for the voiceless)
O (Overturn injustices)
U (Unlock doors of freedom)
R (Regain control of your destiny)
A (Alleviate suffering)
G (Glitter through the night)
E (Echo your beliefs in deeds)

Although the goals of the program are supposed to include improved academic learning and teacher-student relationships, implementing a program of this nature is especially inappropriate for younger children. The hidden message seems to be that teachers don't cherish the learning time they have with young children, a most critical element of effective schools.

The happiest students I have ever seen are those who are learning and succeeding. Children learn kindness and ethical behaviors from parents and modeling by adults and teachers as they focus on academics.

Above all, if you are concerned with CRT programs, take your concerns and expectations directly to school boards. They exist to serve students and parents!

Parents must take the time to understand what is happening in America's elementary schools. It is important to attend school board meetings and not be afraid to make your opinions known. You are responsible for the education of your children. Elect school board members who care about student performance and make decisions based on how their decisions affect your children.

Request that you be placed on school board agendas or make your feelings known in the call to the public portion of a school board meeting. Doing so does not suggest that you are a "domestic terrorist!"

Elementary schools do not have the instructional time to devote to the teaching of anything other than the most important skills that will help our children become literate. *The Longest Pandemic* has attempted to show how every minute of allocated instruction is important. Schools need more time to devote to the basic subjects of reading, grammar, spelling, math, and penmanship, particularly in the first years of school.

Primary level children have brains that are like sponges and have the ability to absorb and process a lot of information. It seems illogical to me to introduce information that could make children feel sad about themselves, whether white, black, or other. Our schools should be founded on the philosophy that all children are precious and equal in God's eyes.

In my opinion, the CRT movement has perpetuated divisions in our country, and it is educational malpractice to broach the subject with young children. Yet the National Education Association (NEA), the largest labor union in the United States, has endorsed the addition of CRT in education.[48]

Do teachers' unions and associations even understand what creates educational excellence in America's schools? My feelings are that they're most interested in their own philosophies and resist being active players in helping to improve the education of our children.

Fortunately, the inclusion of CRT in schools seems to have awoken parents, many of whom have become actively involved in the issue by making their opposition views known.

We must re-examine the purpose of our schools. Over the years the need to produce excellent academic skills has slowly been eroded because of political issues. We should revisit the purpose of our elementary schools and throw out everything except teaching basic skills. Any good teacher will inherently help children understand how to be an ethical person and that it is important to be a good role model and treat all human beings with kindness and understanding.

I would be weary of curriculum efforts, such as the 1619 Project originating from the *New York Times* and named for the date of the first arrival of Africans on American soil.[49] The project aims to reframe the country's history by placing the consequences of slavery at the center of our national narrative. While some may claim it is just a "piece of journalism," I believe it supports the concepts formulated in CRT.

My favorite history teacher recently reminded me that he taught his students about the horrors of slavery and the contributions of many important Black Americans. There is so much more to American history that is important. Does it put ideology ahead of historical understanding?

The Zinn Education Project supports reparations. Black Lives Matter and the African American Policy Forum are organizations that believe there is a need to address structural inequality and systematic oppression. These organizations actively work to include their philosophies in schools, something I feel erodes the basic purpose of our elementary schools.

Gender Identity Issues

The recent issue of gender identification typifies just how crazy the situation has gotten in some of our public schools. Frankly, the latest effort to teach our youngest children about sexual identity makes me nuts! Educators should leave raising children to parents. There is no time or place in American education for such nonsense, especially in elementary education. Although teachers are responsible for the education and safety of children, they are not parents. They have no right to deal with issues of sexuality in innocent young children. Having "drag queens" in schools makes me sick. How can anyone think this is good for the education of students, particularly at the elementary level? What is wrong with those schools encouraging this program of behavior?

In my opinion, those types of actions are immoral. Additionally, less than 1 percent of America's population is transgender, yet some schools and some teachers seem intent on addressing the issue in elementary schools. Parents need to continue to get more involved and understand what is happening in our schools!

Chapter 22

PHONICS AND READING INSTRUCTION

I *cannot overemphasize* the importance of phonics in reading instruction, particularly with new readers in the primary elementary grades. Although I have seen some movement in education towards the inclusion of more phonics elements in elementary classrooms, most school programs do not provide the systematic phonics emphasis needed.

The original problem with phonics instruction began many years ago with the gradual movement by book companies toward whole language and the look-say-word memory. Enthusiasts somehow seemed to be prisoners of a litany of phonics "myths." Fortunately, I was guided by educational research that dismissed those myths. One of the most important research articles ever written should be required reading in all university elementary teacher-training programs. Patrick Groff, a professor of education at San Diego State University wrote *Preventing Reading Failure: An Examination of Myths of Reading Instruction.*[50] Some of these myths are as follows:

The teaching of phonics hinders the development of children's reading comprehension. There is significant educational research that dispels this myth. In fact, research evidence suggests the best results in reading for meaning is achieved in reading programs that emphasize phonics.

English is spelled so unpredictably that phonics has limited usefulness. Groff's own study shows that there is greater usefulness to be found in the teaching of phonics. The English language is phonetic-based, and learning the sounds of letters or combinations of letters is critical in understanding words. If the application of phonics rules results in approximate pronunciations of words, young children can infer and reproduce their true pronunciations.

Children should be taught to read words as "wholes." In fact, the teaching of "sight" words has been discredited by educational research.

Beginning reading is best taught in sentences. There is no convincing evidence that this sentence method results in better reading development than is possible with the use of intensive teaching of phonics.

Context clues are useful as a mode of word recognition. Remember pictures in the Dick and Jane reading materials? The reading company used both this and the previous myth in their basal programs. Research actually shows that the use of context clues too soon and too intensively will create an undesirable dependence on beginning readers and can hinder their overall reading growth.

Word length is not significant in beginning reading instruction. This myth addresses the use of words with more than one syllable. The length of a word significantly influences the difficulty encountered by beginning readers.

The ability to read is dependent on a child's learning style (auditory or visual learners.) This has never been proven in beginning reading situations. Although many teachers still believe strongly in this myth, it is an unproven supposition. In reality, multisensory instruction is more important, especially in early reading programs and, in fact, research indicates intensive phonics teaching should be made available to all students.

The teaching of letter names is unimportant in beginning reading programs. Letter names must be known in order to be useful in the recognition of words.

Reading tests do not truly measure reading ability. It is not a surprise that teachers do not generally support testing and performance standards, especially when children taught using phonics programs clearly outperformed those children taught by other methods. In general, teachers are not supportive of testing programs even though testing programs provide useful information on student reading performance.

Throughout *The Longest Pandemic,* I have mentioned several terms that I think should be clarified. The general term *phonics* refers to the instruction in the association of speech sounds with printed symbols. Systematic phonics is a method that follows a carefully selected sequence of letter-to-sound relationships, organized into a logical order. Phonemic awareness is the ability to hear, identify, and manipulate individual sounds in spoken words.

The Spalding Program "Writing Road to Reading"

The Spalding "Writing Road to Reading" is one of the most effective programs I have seen.[51] The Spalding program was used for reading and writing in the fundamental school. It is not a "canned" or basal book program but more of a carefully designed teaching process. The Spalding Method is a phonics-based reading and writing program. The program integrates phonograms (the sounds of letters or groups of letters) with penmanship. Emphasis is placed on spelling and original writing in the program.

The Spalding Program was developed by Romalda and Walter Spalding and included the research of Dr. Samuel T. Orton, a neuropsychiatrist who was interested in how the brain functions in learning a language.[52] Dr. Orton came to the conclusion that early intervention creates an equal and optimal educational opportunity for every student. The program supports extended hours of language instruction in the primary grades.

In the fundamental school all children, including limited English-speaking and learning-disabled students, were able to get extra help with phonics by participating in the resource program after school. The extra assistance with the Spalding Program eliminated the need for expensive basal texts and workbooks. In upper elementary grades, the program was used for spelling, handwriting, and vocabulary development.

One of the advantages of the program is it can be used with groups of children. Some teachers break up their classes into smaller groups to help accommodate different reading levels, thus minimizing student to teacher direct interaction. However, creating small groups by reading ability led me to the conclusion that children were receiving significantly less direct instruction. I have seen primary teachers working with as many as six small reading groups of children in their classroom, giving them only 15 or 20 minutes of direct instruction for each small group. While they taught the small groups (or centers as they are often called) the rest of the students were given independent studies. This never made sense to me because it limited actual reading instruction, although I appreciated the effort and work teachers had to individualize their instruction by creating smaller reading groups.

The Spalding program requires training for all the teachers to implement the program. The fundamental school allowed and even encouraged parents to participate in the training. As a result, they were able to provide instructional assistance to the children who needed a little extra help at home. This was especially important for new students who were not familiar with the fundamental school's Spalding program. The resource program also provided an excellent opportunity for children requiring remedial help, including Title I students (a federal remedial reading and math program). Children with former learning disabled labels flourished in the fundamental program, especially with tutoring help provided in the resource program.

I do not consider myself an expert in teaching English to these children, although I held a Structured English Immersion Certificate required in Arizona and previously conducted doctoral research in the achievement testing of limited English and non-English-speaking first graders. I can tell you that the limited English-speaking children in the first-grade fundamental pilot program functioned very well and were on or well above grade level by the time the required testing program was administered in the spring.

The English and Spanish languages are phonetic. My wife, a Spanish speaker, tells me that Spanish was easier for her because the Spanish vowels only have one sound. Could it be that the English language is less confusing to Spanish dominant speakers because it incorporates the principles of sound-to-symbol correspondence?

I visited the fundamental school students many times during the pilot program. Some of the initial reactions of the teachers in the Spalding training were not positive. A few teachers expressed the concern that teaching the phonograms in the Spalding Program would be boring. I observed exactly the opposite from the students. They enjoyed reciting the sounds of the phonograms when presented with practice flash cards. Also important was the program's multisensory nature, using what is termed "pathways to the mind" that includes sight, sound, voice, and writing. This addresses some current issues with the ability to read and write legibly.[53]

Spalding students become much better spellers and more capable writers!

The State Superintendent of Public Instruction and one of the longest-serving members of the Arizona House of Representatives, both were especially interested in education, visited one of my elementary schools in northeast Arizona, close to the Navajo Reservation. They were amazed at the content, spelling, grammar, and handwriting of my primary Navajo students. I will never forget their comment while walking down the hall reviewing posted student writing work, especially since we had just begun to use the Spalding Program. "This is amazing work for third-grade students," to which I replied, "But that is the work of our first graders!"

Implementation of the Spalding method in reading and writing instruction requires forty-five hours of training. The fundamental teachers were paid stipends to attend the training. The teachers participating in the program were assured that the children's performance would improve dramatically if they implemented the program as designed. I believe some of the reading programs currently being marketed can be taught by a completely novice person as long as they follow the instructions in the program. That does not speak highly for dedicated teachers. The fundamental teachers learned how effective the Spalding program was after they actually used the program and began to see incredible student growth.

Could it be possible that the need for an extra week of training may have been one of the reasons the Spalding program in the fundamental school was eliminated? Providing the Spalding Method training positively impacted the performance of the students in the school and, in the long term, saved the district significant fiscal resources.

After the first day of training, a new teacher (eventually a curriculum director in another school district) told me, "Dr. D, I believe in what you are trying to accomplish, but I have never seen anything like this. I don't like it because it looks like it's going to be very hard to learn. It also seems boring." I encouraged her to use the program as trained, come back after a couple of months of teaching, and give me an honest evaluation of the program. Late in the fall, that same teacher told me she was astonished at the progress her students were making. "My children are reading and writing at a level I never thought possible!"

The publications *Becoming a Nation of Readers*[54] and *First Lessons*[55] support instructional programs that include systematic, intensive, direct, and beginning phonics in the teaching of reading skills.

The Spalding "Reading Road to Writing" Program teaches phonograms in conjunction with penmanship (a subject deemphasized in American primary education) to help develop spelling skills that lead to original writing experiences. It emphasizes the reading of original writing and the reading of printed material. All of these elements unify the language arts program. The program uses a multisensory methodology that addresses what has been called "learning styles." That is, it provides visual, auditory, and kinesthetic strategies in reading and writing instruction.

A four-year study by Arizona State University showed students taught with the Spalding "Writing Road to

Reading" method had significantly higher test scores when compared to those students taught by mainstream reading programs.[56] The study included 1,000 kindergarten to third-grade students, half of which were taught using mainstream reading programs and half using the Spalding Program. All of the students were tested three times using the Dynamic Indicators of Basic Early Literacy Skills (DIBELS) testing program.[57]

The DIBELS test was developed through the auspices of the University of Oregon Center on Teaching and Learning. It includes a set of procedures and measures for quickly assessing the acquisition of early literacy skills. DIBELS was developed to measure the reading literacy of what are considered the most important reading skills. Those skills include letter naming fluency, phonemic-segmentation fluency, nonsense-word fluency, word-reading fluency, and oral-reading fluency. The test also measures advanced phonics and word attack skills, accuracy, fluent reading of the connected text, and reading comprehension.

Individual testing is quickly administered with a reading comprehension test also administered individually in just a few minutes. DIBELS is a formal and standardized testing program being used by some schools in the United States. Schools that use the DIBELS assessments are focusing on those skills important in reading instruction, most importantly in the primary elementary grades. The DIBELS test provides an effective way to quickly determine individual children's needs and skills. This is particularly important considering the current mobility of parents and children from one school to another.

Some schools, particularly in inner cities, have a very high rate of student mobility. Teachers need a quick method to determine instructional needs when new students are registered.

The Spalding program students have consistently higher average values in all DIBELS test areas, providing clear evidence that the Spalding Program is better than schools using other reading programs, most of which are published by large book companies. The improvement in student achievement scores is significant and dramatic. Spalding connects speech to print rather than print to speech, thus allowing children to firstly concentrate on hearing the sounds in spoken words.

Children who struggle to hear or manipulate sounds in spoken words have trouble decoding words. In the Spalding program, phonemic awareness is coordinated with teaching the letter combinations that represent speech sounds. Any college teacher education program that does not teach their students this process exacerbates an instructional problem because they do not necessarily teach research-based reading methods to their students.

Much reading research has been created through the work of the U.S. Department of Education and the National Institute of Child Health and Human Development, which formed the National Reading Panel.[58] The panel reviewed an incredible amount of research information to help determine the most effective reading instruction methods. The panel's analysis made it clear that the best approach to reading instruction is one that incorporates explicit instruction in phonemic awareness, systematic phonics, methods to improve fluency, and ways to enhance comprehension.

Entire reading problems became seriously challenged in the reading wars, especially in the 80's. Rudolph Flesch was again brought into the issue with a *Reader's Digest* article by Edward Ziegler subtitled "Why Our Children Aren't Reading."[59] It summarized the efforts and history of Dr. Flesch and the *Reader's Digest* version that read "Look, Dick, look. Look why Dick can't read. Dick can't read if he's taught like this."

Why isn't the issue solved, and why don't our schools use phonics programs to the extent schools did 60 years ago?

Parents should check to see what reading programs are used in their schools and ask how teachers are able to measure progress in mastering reading skills.

In reading studies, the differences regarding phonics are dramatic and statistically significant. Unfortunately, many colleges of education do not provide research-based instruction that teachers need to effectively teach all children to read.

One of the best principals I have known told me that her district recruits Arizona State University's (ASU) education graduates because the university produces better teachers. It is apparent to me that the Technology Based Learning and Research entity at ASU has been very successful because its teacher-training program focuses on research-based instruction.[60]

So is this just old-school propaganda? A review of 2019 elementary school labels and rankings given to all of the state's elementary schools helps provide the answer.[61] All the elementary schools using phonics-based reading programs were highly ranked.

I was writing part of this book while sitting in a hospital. My wife's nurse, knowing I was a former school superintendent, told me she was concerned about what school she should enroll her soon-to-be-school-age child. After telling me where she lived, I helped her by doing a quick Internet search and looked at all of the neighborhood schools in her school district.[62] It was not surprising that the performance of one school was outstanding and the best in her district. The students in that school are taught using a phonics-based language arts program. The school is a traditional magnet school in a district of 23 other elementary schools close to her home in Phoenix, Arizona. She was very happy for the help, and I was not in the least bit surprised with the results of my quick search. The nurse was amazed that it was so easy to find a good school!

I spent many hours looking for effective language arts programs. My interest was in general performance and instructional programming. I was specifically interested in the rankings for elementary schools using phonics programs and, in particular, the Spalding Program. It is interesting that there are only about a dozen elementary schools in Arizona that have been accredited by the Spalding Foundation even though there are many other schools using the program. Accreditation requires extensive evidence that the school staff have met rigorous external standards for the Spalding Method of language arts instruction. Spalding teacher training is accredited by the International Multi-Sensory Structured

Language Education Council and the International Dyslexia Association and focuses on essential skills and behaviors identified by the National Reading Panel and the Knowledge and Practice Standards for Teachers of Reading.[63]

Having had some experience using Spalding programming, I learned that effective Spalding teachers need experience and continuous training to become truly proficient in the use of the program. Completing the initial training does create a challenge for districts and schools. The time for training and funding for the program, not to mention the funds to pay teachers to participate in the training, can be problematic. However, parents would be shocked if they knew the per pupil costs of most elementary school reading programs.

In the fundamental school's case, the use of the program did save thousands of dollars. The average cost for some reading programs is unconscionable. The marketing of reading programs is a huge business for publishers. The costs for the Spalding Reading Road to Writing program easily offset the cost of other book company programs. This is particularly important in an age when funding for education is limited. After I completed my look at Spalding schools, I was not surprised to conclude the following:

1. The Spalding accredited elementary schools are A-rated and ranked very high in the information provided by the Arizona Department of Education and SchoolDigger.com.

2. Accreditation by the Spalding Foundation is impressive but has not prevented other elementary schools from using the program.
3. Ranking information showed that these schools were among the very best in the state, with most ranked in the top 50 schools in Arizona.
4. The numerous other schools using the program were also highly ranked elementary schools, all of which received A ratings by the Arizona (noting that any elementary school ranked in the top 10 percent of schools would receive a ranking somewhere in the top one hundred elementary schools).

After the first year of the pilot fundamental school, I compared the fundamental school students' achievement scores (Iowa Test of Basic Skills) to the other schools in Arizona as well as the comprehension scores of Arizona and national test scores in reading comprehension.

Fundamental School Reading Comprehension Scores (National Percentile Scores):

Grade 1- One of the best scores in Arizona (90th percentile)
Grade 2- One of the best scores in Arizona (90th percentile)
Grade - One of the best scores in Arizona (90th percentile)
Grade 4- One of the best scores in Arizona (90th percentile)
Grade 5- One of the best scores in Arizona (85th percentile)
Grade 6- One of the best scores in Arizona (87th percentile)

Arizona averages at the time were approximately in the 40th to 48th percentile!

National averages at the time were approximately in the 45th to 50th percentile![64]

As you might notice, average scores are now much lower than the scores produced years ago.

These scores eliminated any worries regarding reading comprehension. I learned the children developed excellent decoding skills that help raise the comprehension of written materials!

We encouraged the fundamental teachers to use classic literature with the program and did purchase used Open Court Program books because they contained abundant classic literature. You will find a wonderful list of classic literature if you are interested in what reading materials are recommended in the Spalding program and the former Westside Preparatory Academy. It is an incredible list of literature. We purchased Open Court's used books because of cost savings.

When my own girls were young, I spent many hours reading stories that included the Grimm Fairy Tales. As a young parent and teacher, I was particularly impressed with the paperback *The Uses of Enchantment – The Meaning and Importance of Fairy Tales* by the child psychologist Bruno Bettelheim.[65] While Bettelheim was more interested in the psychology of fairy tales and the lessons the tales played in the child's developmental psyche, I was more interested in the depth of the vocabulary in fairy tales and, later, all classic literature. There is great value in the lessons fairy tales convey to children.

I remember one of the book salesmen who presented his company's reading program to the teachers and parents. He proudly told them that his program "Carefully limited the difficulty of the vocabulary in their program." I was a little concerned with that statement and later completed my own analysis of the difficulty of the words contained in their program as well as the words contained in fairy tales and classic literature. Using an analysis of the number of syllables in the words, the number of multi-syllabic words, and the numbers of those words in the sentences, it helped me approximate the difficulty of the vocabulary and reading materials.

The book salesman was accurate as their materials did limit the use of more difficult words and the sentence length in initial reading instruction. As a result of that analysis, we chose to use the Spalding Writing Road to Reading in combination with classic literature because we did not necessarily want to limit vocabulary.

"Fine books fill the minds of students with a wealth of knowledge – of character and philosophy, of history and science, of humor and wit."[66]

Phonograms

"Now the way to learn any such system is to learn to write and read at the same time. And how do you do that? The obvious answer is by taking up one symbol after another and learning how to write it and how to recognize it. Once you are through the whole list of symbols, you can read and write; the rest is simply practice – learning to do it more and more automatically."[67] The Spalding Program begins with intensive phonics. The English alphabet and language is phonetic and uses a sound symbol system.

There are 26 letters in our alphabet with 45 different sounds. In addition, there are 70 common phonograms that should be taught daily. Children are drilled with the phonograms and spell those sounds on paper, while incorporating proper penmanship skills. The phonograms are letters and combinations of letters that create voice sounds for words.

After teaching the initial consonant sounds, vowel sounds are taught. Children are then taught rules using paired phonograms. Children are taught a total of 110 combinations of sounds with the phonograms that they should master in the first quarter of the school year. They are drilled every day with the phonograms and their sounds or combinations of sounds. While this may sound boring to non-Spalding teachers, the children loved the drills and enjoyed success in mastering the phonograms and their sounds.

Many children simply cannot write legibly because they have not been taught how to write. The Spalding Program stresses proper penmanship and even teaches children how to properly hold a pencil. Good penmanship requires practice and should continue throughout the elementary school years. It begins with printing and continues until students begin to connect the printed letters with cursive writing. Even kindergarten students possess the fine motor skills needed to begin to print properly. Unfortunately, penmanship programs are practically nonexistent in many elementary schools!

I have never seen such poor penmanship in students because teachers have deemphasized the importance of penmanship in the elementary grades.

I remember being graded on neatness and even remember penmanship cards with the proper printing and writing of letters pinned to the wall above classroom chalkboards. I attended a parochial school and remember practicing writing as we began to move into cursive writing. I still like visiting old schools and am amazed that many abandoned classrooms and old schoolhouses still have those penmanship cards pinned to the wall above chalkboards.

In later grades, those cards began to illustrate proper cursive letters, and we were expected to use them in writing assignments. "Small errors prevent children from learning to write easily, legibly, and neatly. They require careful and continued teaching of all the techniques. From the beginning, children need to be taught directives. Success in these writing skills gives children great pride and interest in learning each day's lesson. Each skill builds self-confidence."[68]

According to Dr. Mosse's book, *The Complete Handbook of Children's Reading Disorders* "Careful clinical examination of children can disentangle all the different factors involved in the causation of reading disorders and can provide a valid basis for practical and useful diagnostic categories, the only realistic guidelines enabling treatment and prevention."[69] She is a formidable advocate of the Spalding Program. Her book included the clinical observation of many beginning readers. Her works also included comprehensive psychological tests of children, studies of families and including siblings, and studies of the socioeconomic factors that might have been factors in her studies of children. She lists several additional benefits of teaching reading through writing with Spalding and other similar techniques.

According to Dr. Mosse, the child's pronunciation of formal English improves. The "Technique makes it possible to teach children from the beginning that slight differences in sound, as well as the different spelling of sounds, change the meaning of words."[70] Many children remember new words when they write them down, emphasizing the importance of writing in the reading process.

The book *Preventing Reading Difficulties in Young Children*[71] supports the importance of phonics in early reading programs. "For children learning an alphabetic language, like English, there is an important additional ingredient: phonological awareness and, in particular, phonemic awareness."

So why are phonics programs so inexcusably absent in so many public school programs?

I am also an advocate of teaching some keyboarding skills to upper elementary school grades when students have the physical skills to use the keyboard. It is an important skill that is critical in this age of technology. In high school we were required to take typing, a skill I still use every single day.

It is amazing to watch young people texting on their smartphones. One day I decided to test the texting skills of a random sample of high school students. Smartphones had already become an important staple in the lives of older students. I was very interested in phone texting as a high school principal, so one day I randomly chose six students and asked them to copy one written page with their cell phones. After a minute I evaluated their texts and was amazed to see that the six students were able to correctly type more than 40 words in a minute without error. Reflecting on my high school typing class experience, I remember being proud of my 43 words per minute and the grade I received for the effort. Although I remain concerned about the use of smartphones at such an early age, students have evolved such that they have some really useful skills. Wow, times have changed!

The history of activities noted in *The Longest Pandemic* happened in the 80's. Teachers in those years placed more emphasis on penmanship and writing in elementary programs. The use of detailed penmanship instruction in today's elementary instruction is now virtually nonexistent. I believe it is still a critical element of instruction. At that time elementary schools began to abandon the traditional "stick ball" method of penmanship in favor of the introduction of script writing in the early stages of penmanship instruction. Teachers have begun to favor more creativity and imagination in writing, giving less attention to actual grammar, penmanship, and spelling.

One of the biggest complaints I continue to hear from parents today is "My child has terrible handwriting." That complaint is accompanied by parents who tell me "My child can't spell."

Other Phonics Programs

I remember the negative teacher perceptions and jokes teachers made about the advertised program "Hooked on Phonics" in 1987. I told them that they should look at what the program was selling and think about their own programs. Perhaps the company was filling a void.

The company's initial sales exceeded $100 million dollars per year. After a series of problems, the company was transferred to Educate, Inc., who operated Sylvan Learning and has added additional programs such as "Hooked on Handwriting" and "Hooked on Spelling." Now acquired by Sandviks, the program has been downloaded 500,000 times. In its advertising program, the company states that the latest version of the program has materials designed to help support every learning style and provides a guarantee that the learner will improve one grade level in just a month. Perhaps public schools should provide some type of guarantee!

My elementary teachers were all nuns who included at least a half hour of daily phonics instruction. When reading is connected to phonics students learn important skills not learned through phonics in isolation. The teaching of phonics has proven to produce higher reading skills, especially with students who have a strong foundation in their early education. A systematic approach to teaching phonics is more effective than non-systematic approaches and even helps prevent reading disorders. A systematic method follows a carefully selected sequence of letter-sound relationships organized into a logical order.

There are many schools (including charters) that use phonics programs. Many of the most successful schools utilize systematic phonics programs in their instruction. Reading First Schools teach phonics and my neighbor's younger children attend the Challenger Basic School in Gilbert, Arizona, a very good school that uses the Spalding

Method in their program. They are very pleased with their children's academic growth and are very supportive of the school.

Parents should make sure to ask the administration of their school if they include phonics programs in their reading instruction, particularly in the early grades.

Searching the Internet, you will find an incredible number of other phonics programs. The "Hooked on Phonics" method is still available as a complete kit and available in digital format. Both options come with access to a mobile application that includes video, interactive games, and eBooks. The complete kit also comes with workbooks and the program serves prekindergarten through second-grade children. The program is highly rated by parents, and this would be especially effective in home study situations.

"Zoo-Phonics" is another program and, according to those knowledgeable, believe it is a "robust and well designed" program. "Explore the Code" is a more traditional phonics program. It is important to note that phonics instruction should be connected to reading and has shown to be more effective in teaching students to decode words. Students who are able to decode unknown words will be stronger readers. The "Reading First" and "Reading Street" programs favor phonics and phonemic awareness. Other instructional programs include "Reading Reels" that provides embedded multimedia in daily lessons and "Writing to Read" which combines technology and non-technology small group activities.

"Success for All" is a comprehensive school reform effort designed to help ensure success in reading for children in high-poverty schools. The highly rated "Direct Instruction" is an approach to beginning reading instruction that emphasizes a step-by-step approach to phonics and decodable texts that make use of a teaching alphabet and a scripted manual for teachers. Several schools enhance reading achievement using computer-assisted instruction in phonics and phonological awareness.

Some programs are built using a cooperative learning philosophy such as "Success for All," "Peer-Assisted Learning Strategies," "Reading Reels," and "Class Wide Peer Tutoring." All of these programs address phonics issues. The "Open Court" program has shown to be effective and requires professional development for teachers, something I find important if the reading instruction is to be effective.

Other phonics-based programs include "Scholastic Phonics Readers," "Phonics in Context," "Destination Reading," "Headsprout," "Plato Focus," "Waterford Early Reading Program," "Phonics Based Reading," "The Literacy Center (Leap Frog)," "Reading Machine," "Reading Reels," "Sing Spell Read Write," "Early Reading Research," "Reading and Integrated Literacy Strategies," "Ladders to Literacy," "Orton-Gillingham," "Four Blocks," "Superkids," and "Voyager Universal Literacy." I have not evaluated any of these programs. There are many other phonics programs available that are too numerous to list. I am sure some are better than others, and I am not endorsing any of the programs mentioned. I am simply endorsing the use of phonics instruction in reading. Other phonics programs not mentioned may be effective. The increasing number of available programs indicates the importance that many people feel about phonics instruction.

Ask your school how they determine the individual needs of each child and how they intend to meet all of the children's instructional needs! Whatever you do, insist that your school includes systematic phonics instruction. Do not settle for anything less!

Chapter 23

After Eliminating the Fundamental Program

I examined the specific performance of the former fundamental school prior to the pandemic in 2019 because of the concerns I have for the lower student performance versus the very high achievement of the original school. According to the website SchoolDigger.com, the school ranked 709 of the total 1029 schools in Arizona. Their two-star rating (out of a possible five stars) and C label ranked worse than 68.9 percent of elementary schools in Arizona. It also ranked sixth of the eight ranked schools in the district. The student-teacher ratio of 23:1 is lower than that of the original school student-to-teacher ratio of 25:1 students in each classroom.[72]

NICHE.com gives the school an overall C grade, a B- in academics, a B for the teaching staff, and a B- for diversity.[73] They advertise state test scores, indicating that 35 percent of the school's students are at least proficient in math and 40 percent in reading. Zillow.com uses older data on their website, stating that 34 percent of the students are limited English-speaking and give the school a rating of 5 out of 10.[74] The school has slowly slipped into mediocrity after it abandoned a program that was built on best practices information and effective school research.

Every state in the nation has an educational website sponsored by their departments of education. There is a great deal of data available for every one of the elementary schools in each state and I would encourage parents to use the Internet to search for information from your state department of education. As an example, excellent data is published in the Arizona State Department of Education Website AZ School Report Card describing awards and recognition, academic offerings, music and art programs, after-school opportunities, and a description of each school facility.[75] Trying to absorb this much information can be a little daunting, but state education websites provide excellent data.

The former fundamental school has a number of teachers with emergency teaching certification that indicates they are lacking some requirements for permanent certification. Arizona has tightened its certification process in the past few years and the number of non-certified teachers can be problematic for schools. The process used to assign letter grades to each school is extensive. Individual yearly school profiles provided are required in Arizona and designed to measure student academic growth, proficiency in English language arts, math and science, and academic growth of English language learners.

While each state is different, valuable information is readily available everywhere in the nation. Parents can review a myriad of data available from various websites, but I caution parents to be careful with some private websites, which are designed to provide real estate options for parents.

Chapter 24

SCHOOL ADMINISTRATION

School administrators and others responsible for managing the education of our elementary school youth are supposed to be leaders. Many superintendents have good public relations skills. They dress well, shake hands, and smile, while trying to make their schools look good, even in situations where student performance is questionable and other problems abound. More importantly, long-tenured superintendents are exceptionally good at managing school boards and that certainly helps with job security. There is additional job security for administrators that can keep teachers happy. However, school board and staff satisfaction is not necessarily congruent with instructional effectiveness.

The performance of a district and the evaluation of its leadership should always include the factor of student achievement.

Many of the principals and superintendents that can make a difference in instructional quality lack one vitally important characteristic. They seem resistant to look at programs that are proven successful or outstanding by any measurable criteria, especially student performance. Far too many are hesitant to "rock the boat."

Looking for successful programs or understanding effective school research and proven success seems to be the easiest way to help improve programming. They should look to districts that have the best student performance and try to learn what they are doing to help create excellent student performance.

Some administrators have insufficient practical or educational knowledge to know what works best. Years ago, successful athletic coaches were often moved into leadership positions and particularly into school principal positions. Many became principals because they were proven disciplinarians or winners on the field. This situation isn't so prevalent today, but I can relate to the situation.

My first public school position was as a secondary science and social studies teacher. I taught geomorphology, mineralogy, earth science, and world geography in high school. As a former coach, my principal seemed most interested in athletic success. Fortunately, his assistant principal was concerned with instructional effectiveness and visited my classroom regularly. He gave me many excellent strategies to help improve my instruction.

My first administrative position was as an assistant elementary principal in a very large school. At that time my previous experience was exclusively secondary education. My initial feelings of terror about being assigned to an elementary program were heightened by the superintendent's concern for the performance of the current principal. He believed the school needed better organization, improved teacher evaluation, and better student discipline. When I questioned my own lack of experience at the elementary level, I was told that my qualifications and references from the university would enable me to succeed at the elementary level. I was also told to closely evaluate one specific teacher whom he deemed "The worst teacher he had ever seen." Apparently, evaluating teachers was not the existing principal's most important priority, but she was one of the hardest workers I have ever seen. Her greatest attribute was her love of children.

My first administrative position turned out to be a valuable learning experience. The teacher I was told to carefully evaluate was, although a fine human being, was actually one of the worst teachers I have ever seen. After a year of frustrating evaluations and interactions, the teacher resigned and became a successful developer and realtor. Years later, he thanked me for my evaluations and told me "Resigning from my teaching position was the best thing that ever happened to me. I am happy now and have made more money than I could have ever imagined. I am really good at my current job and know I was not a good teacher, hated my job and glad you helped change my life." I will never forget the conversation and remain thankful for his comments. What a learning experience!

After years of excellent elementary school experience, I returned to the university to finish a doctoral program. I loved the elementary students and teachers in my initial administrative position, but was far from becoming a good principal. My first elementary principal position was in one of the highest-performing elementary schools in the state. I worked hard to make the school even better and learned what it takes to be a good leader. I always looked at the students' academic performance in comparison to the other high performing schools and worked hard to help keep my school at the highest possible level.

The opportunity to apply what I had learned through experience came a couple of years later when I was hired as an assistant superintendent in an elementary school district serving kindergarten through eighth-grade students. That position gave me the opportunity to put in place effective school research work and the ideas I thought would help make the district's schools more successful. The opportunity to help create the fundamental school changed my professional life for the better and forms much of the information contained in *The Longest Pandemic*.

Merit Pay in the Educational Establishment

I believe in merit pay for administrators and teachers because performance is important if we are to improve education in our country. Educators have the duty to produce functionally literate students, so why should it not be an element considered in compensation programs? America is a capitalist nation, and performance is critical in most private sector establishments, so why not public education? I have seen far too many incredibly poor administrators and teachers making so much more than less experienced but more capable employees.

It is possible for a school board to create valuable goals and then ask the administration to address those goals by establishing very specific objectives, all of which can be quantified into a merit system.

I developed and implemented a merit pay system for administrators and it not only helped keep the school board and community updated on progress at every board meeting, but also helped keep the administration focused on meeting their objectives and, ultimately, the school board's goals.

Chapter 25

PARENT STRATEGIES TO HELP CHOOSE THE BEST SCHOOL

Principal or Teacher Interview

Districts usually have mandatory attendance zones for their schools. I would encourage parents to look carefully at your neighborhood school as well as other alternatives, including public, private, parochial, or charter schools. In view of the funding source for schools and their reliance on full-time equivalency funding, it is possible that other districts or even schools outside the parents' district of attendance will accept students, particularly if parents are willing to provide transportation. Some school districts are even running transportation routes outside of their district or school boundaries.

The competition to increase enrollment can be furious. Charter schools are tuition-free and always a possible alternative, and scholarships may be available for higher achieving students or athletes in parochial schools.

A helpful strategy in choosing a school is to interview the teacher or principal. The following interview questions are provided as a tool if you choose the interview strategy. While public schools may be your only alternative, the following interview questions may help you familiarize yourself with the school. The interview questions will at least provide parents with information about the quality of a school and give educators notice that you are concerned about the education your child is to receive.

Schools often schedule a "parent-night" to discuss their school program. I would not wait for parent nights that are often scheduled well after school begins. However, you can also use these questions at a parent-night program. If the school administration does not honor your request for an interview or at least provide a program information night where you can ask questions, consider other alternatives.

Questions for the school administrator:

1. Would you allow me to visit your school to get more familiar with your program?

If the answer is no, consider alternatives. A good school should welcome your interest. Try to stay in the background and be especially careful to follow all conditions and school rules required by the school. Listen and look carefully!

2. Would you allow me to spend time observing the grade level teachers for my child?

The answer should absolutely be yes. This is an especially important question if you are new to the school. The school may wish to establish conditions for your visit, but it is important to visit as many teachers as possible. Visiting more than one classroom will give administrators the impression that you are attempting to evaluate and choose your child's teacher. As a parent, you have the right to request a teacher and it is always better to put all requests in writing. I encourage parents to be aware of the students' general performance in each class, information that is available. Really good teachers have a well-deserved reputation. Your efforts should be to get your child in the best possible program.

Note: As a former elementary principal in one of the highest performing elementary schools in the state, the parents' ability to choose a teacher for their children became a huge issue and potential problem for me as a new principal. Parents were very involved in the school. The school demographics included many professional parents who cared deeply about the quality of their children's education.

In this case, the school had one of the best and most effective sixth-grade teachers I have ever known. The children and their parents loved this teacher for many good reasons. The teacher's students significantly outperformed their peers on the state's mandated test and parents routinely reviewed achievement test scores that were published in the summer after each school year. The number of parent requests for this teacher far outnumbered all other requests in the entire school. The previous administration did not necessarily honor parent requests although it seemed to approve requests from the most influential and vocal parents.

Classroom assignment lists were advertised at the beginning of the year and posted on the school's front door. Prior to advertising class lists, the teachers met together to develop classroom lists using factors such as student gender (trying to equalize the number of boys and girls), student performance, and behavior. Not considering parental input was problematic and parents had no influence in the development of student classroom assignments at the school. I brought up the problem with my teachers at the first teacher's meeting before classroom assignments were finalized because I had been inundated with verbal requests for one specific sixth grade teacher. I asked the teachers to work together to continue to develop a preliminary list of classroom student assignments. This helped because there were some legitimate concerns that needed to be addressed. One example included a set of identical twins whose parents specifically wanted them separated as a long-standing practice. There were other examples where students' discipline needed to be addressed. It would be inappropriate to load up any one teacher with students whose behaviors are questionable.

After the preliminary lists were developed and before publication I allowed the teachers to review written parent requests from parents. I discovered many of the parents were not willing to address their concerns or wishes in writing. This allowed me to inform the complaining parents that they failed to respond to my requirement to address their wishes in writing, thus settling the issue before it became more of a problem. I also required the parents to focus on the positive reasons they wanted a particular teacher as I had hoped to avoid specific complaints about other teachers, although such concerns were often legitimate.

I informed the teachers that they should be aware of parent concerns and requests. I hoped the teachers would look to their peers for assistance in strategies that helped magnify parent support, and this resulted in a greater level of teacher collaboration. The fact that the teachers were aware of parent requests encouraged the teachers to be cognizant of their own teaching behaviors and seemed to encourage more cooperation. As an example, the sixth-grade teachers went to the most popular sixth grade teacher to find out what she was doing to get so many requests. They became more interested in strategies she employed to help create the best achievement test scores and parent satisfaction, something I had already done myself.

I had already gone to that very competent sixth-grade teacher and bluntly asked how she was able to create such popularity and great achievement test scores. Her response was something I have never forgotten. "Dr. Dallabetta, we use a reading program adopted by the school, correct? Well, I happen to know what skills are consistently tested and make sure I concentrate on those skills in my program in spite of what is taught in the adopted instructional materials." This may have been one of the most significant and eye-opening conversations in my entire career. I have never forgotten the need to make sure the instructional program emphasizes skills that are tested. Is teaching to the test problematic? I don't think so because required tests normally include the most important skills.

3. If you are allowed to visit the classrooms and school, look for the following.

Does the teacher have the ability to keep the students engaged? Do the children behave?

How does the teacher handle students who misbehave?

Is any time wasted during your visit?

Is the teacher the center of instruction during your visit?

Compare classroom achievement prior to your visit. Which teacher achieves the best test results?

Look at the arrangement of the room. Is the classroom traditional with individual student desks? Is there a lot of movement in the classroom or situations that create off-task behaviors?

Are teacher directions easily understood?

How quickly do the students and teacher move between instructional lessons?

Do the children seem to enjoy the classroom?

How much time is allocated for each of the curricular areas of reading, language arts, social studies, and mathematics?

The principal or teacher should be able to give you specific time allocations for each subject. They may express the need to adjust times occasionally but should be able to respond to your question with specifics. In some cases, they may even use percentages or weekly figures. Remember that you need as much information as possible about instruction in reading, language arts, and math. The more specific information they provide regarding the allocation of learning time will give you an idea of their level of control with instruction. If the principal tells you individual decisions on this matter are left to the teacher I would look for another program.

4. **Do you teach penmanship in the primary grades and what program do you use (grades kindergarten through third grade)?**

You should be given a specific answer to this question. This question is especially pertinent to elementary-aged children in the primary grades from kindergarten through grade three. In your interview educators may refer to script writing. Without primary instruction in printing (lower and uppercase letters in "stick ball" format), you should be concerned. If reference is made to "keyboarding" in primary grades I would be even more concerned. While keyboarding skills are critical as children move throughout the grades, penmanship is important and skills that are almost entirely ignored in many elementary schools.

5. Does your beginning reading program include phonics?

Educational research clearly shows that phonics-based reading programs help to create the most capable beginning readers. Make sure you ask for specifics about the reading program. Ask what particular reading program is used and then take the time to learn about that program. If the reading program does not include phonics instruction, look for another school!

6. Does your school and teachers require homework?

The value of homework continues to be controversial. There is no conclusive evidence homework increases student achievement. However, there is a significant amount of research supporting both opinions on the value of homework.[76] Homework seems to be more beneficial to certain groups of students. It appears to have a positive effect on older students because younger students have less effective study habits and are more easily distracted. Further, students from low-income homes may not benefit as much from homework as those from higher-income homes.

As with the original fundamental school philosophy, we felt students would benefit from some homework to help students learn to organize themselves and emphasize the importance of learning. We established specific conditions for homework assignments and teachers were required to review homework. As for elementary students, homework may have other positive benefits such as improved time management, responsibility, study habits, and the ability to stay on task. I believe homework might at least include the requirement to finish classroom assignments at home. Parents should also create a quiet place for students to work. Schools that require some homework appear to have better achievement.

One strategy that I believe addresses some confusion for parents is to limit homework assignments in early grades with more time required as students move through the grades. Parents generally do not understand what is required of specific homework assignments. An excellent approach to homework that helps parents understand homework policies is to create subject and time requirements for each grade. As an example, a first grader may be required to spend 15 minutes with time increasing at each grade level. In the fundamental school homework did not exceed 45 minutes for older students. All students were able to get help with assignments in the fundamental school resource program.

It would be helpful to designate each night to a different subject. For example, Monday might be the reading night where students are required to spend time with independent reading activities. Tuesday night may be mathematics night with other nights designated for studies in writing or other activities.

The important point is to make sure parents understand the homework program and they always know what is required of their children. By designating specific nights and informing parents, they never have to ask their children "Do you have any homework tonight?" They will know what is required and that makes more sense.

7. How do the students in this school perform academically?

The person interviewed should be able to give you a specific answer to any question regarding their school's performance. A school whose entire population consists of minority non-English or limited English speakers is no excuse for poor academic growth. These schools may even have a higher rating because ratings are established, in part, by growth in academic performance from one year to another.

Parents should be concerned about the poor academic performance of a school. If this is the case the school's principal or teacher should be able to explain their plan to deal with poor student performance and school ratings. If not, I would eliminate interest in registering students in schools that consistently have poor school ratings.

8. Does your school provide any art and music programs?

Most schools provide some art and music. I would ask for more specifics if the school provides art and music. Is there an art or music teacher? Does your music program include some type of band program, and what does your art instruction include? An art program should include some formal instructional objectives.

9. What are the instructional objectives in your physical education program?

The fundamental school used the President's Physical Fitness Program. The children were graded on their development and achievement in mastering the skills contained in the program. Rather than throwing out a kickball and letting the children play, the program should include specific objectives geared toward physical development appropriate to each age and grade level. Even the most rigorous physical education programs can be fun for children. The best physical education teacher I ever had was a joy to watch because he emphasized skills, and the children loved his class. He eventually became an excellent school superintendent.

10. How much recess time do you provide to each grade level and what is the recess schedule?

While recess is important, it can have a tremendously negative impact on the quality of the overall instructional program. Mornings are a critical learning time for students. Unfortunately, I have seen schools that begin instruction at 8:30 am and have their first morning recess as early as 9:30 am. Interruptions in the morning are, in my opinion, detrimental to the quality of instruction.

11. Does your school include the use of Critical Race Theory (CRT)?

If the school subscribes to the philosophy of CRT, I would eliminate that school as a choice for your children. I believe the issue simply deepens racial bias and tensions. Ask if the school has a counselor and if their job description involves any direct instruction with children. Any district or school that attempts to introduce CRT in any form should be removed from a school you would consider enrolling children.

A good principal should be very proud of their school and welcome parents' interest and be happy to open the school to visitors. The principal should be able to provide specifics about the program and if not, then consider alternatives.

Chapter 26

MAKING SURE YOUR CHILDREN GET THE BEST!

There are many strategies parents can use to help improve elementary education in their community. Most options are relatively easy but you must show resolve and exert your influence on schools. Getting involved and taking action will help guarantee your children receive the best quality of instruction.

1. Take the time to understand what is being taught in your school.

2. Get involved in your school by reviewing the student performance of your children as well as the performance of children in the entire school. Review website information and understand all options for your children. Don't hesitate to communicate your expectations for your children to the administration and teachers.

3. Elect school board members that understand the importance of student performance. Take steps to

communicate the importance of academic growth to governing board members.

4.   Demand information about the instruction your children receive, including the amount of time allocated for each subject. Ask for specific information about how and what is taught in your school. Make sure you demand reading instruction that includes phonics programs, particularly in the primary grades kindergarten to third grade.

5.   Make sure teachers are teaching children how to write and that penmanship is an important part of the instructional program.

6.   If necessary, seek advocates when you or your children need help. If you don't understand the situation seek assistance from someone who knows education or from competent personnel outside of the school or district.

7.   Don't rely only on conversations you have with school personnel. Document the interactions you have taken with the school or its personnel. Include as much specific information as possible. Don't rely on promises from either administrators or teachers. If you are concerned with the lack of action at the school level teacher or principal make sure you share your concerns with the district office administrators or governing board members.

8. Meet regularly with your children's teacher, particularly if you have concerns. Don't wait for a parent-teacher night at school. Review your own child's progress on a regular basis and make sure you are familiar with your child's progress.

9. Learn what school options you have for the education of your children. There are likely other options that may be better school choices. Look at charter schools in your area and become familiar with optional programming. Use website information and, if appropriate, meet with officials of the school to learn more about instructional programming.

10. Attend school board meetings and get familiar with school district issues. In some cases, you can stream meetings or watch video broadcasts or recordings. Check school board agendas that are posted prior to board meetings. Be especially attentive to "special board" meetings. Attend school board "work" sessions where it might be easier to share your comments and ideas.

11. If your children are referred for "special testing," make sure you understand the special education process. More and more children are being labeled learning disabled and dyslexic when, in fact, they are victims of poor instruction in the primary grades. In many cases, you can seek assistance from your state's education department that may help you as advocates. Seek help if you don't understand the

process. Children who qualify for special education programs must have an Individual Education Plan (IEP). Whatever plan is developed requires your approval and signature. Demand specific instructional goals and make sure your ideas are included in the IEP before formally agreeing to any instructional program.

Chapter 27

SOME RECOMMENDATIONS FOR NEW TEACHERS

Read the first volume of Dr. Hilde Mosse's book *The Complete Handbook of Children's Reading Disorders.*[77] If you are an elementary major, I recommend getting the book and carefully reviewing its contents since teaching reading is one of your most important responsibilities.

Primary Grade Recommendation 1:

Start your reading instruction for beginning students with a strong phonics-based program.[78]

Primary Grade Recommendation 2:

Develop specific time allocations for each subject in your instructional program. It is vitally important that new teachers organize the use of instruction time. Research clearly shows the time spent in instruction is closely correlated to mastery of basic skills. More time spent teaching important reading readiness skills will reap huge rewards for children who are ready to read.

Primary Grade Recommendation 3:

Devote at least 60 percent of your instruction day to reading and language arts skills. This is especially important in the first year of instruction for all children. If your school day is five hours, you should be working on reading and writing skills for at least 2 1/2 to 3 hours per day in kindergarten and first grade.

Primary Grade Recommendation 4:

Teach penmanship skills and help students learn how to print letters of the alphabet in the first few grades before moving children into script writing. Use primary writing paper and work with the children to make sure they are printing correctly.

Primary Grade Recommendation 5:

Reading and writing skills should be taught together. Make sure you include penmanship skills in concert with your phonics instruction.

Elementary School Recommendation 1:

Eliminate wasted time that can be used for instruction. Incorporate teaching methods that encourage on-task behaviors. The more students are actively engaged the more they will learn. Teach children how to efficiently line up for movement within the school. When children return to the classroom make sure you can quickly return to an active learning situation. Ask veteran teachers to share strategies they use to maximize engagement. Limit distractions and student movement in the classroom.

Elementary School Recommendation 2:

Use strategies that help you keep children on task and actively engaged in learning.

Managing behavior is critically important. There are many good programs that help teachers control students. Look at Positive Discipline or Assertive Discipline programs and start each school year making sure your students clearly understand your expectations for behavior. Develop strategies that reward positive behaviors and work towards the consistent use of your behavior management program. Make sure your room is arranged so you are always in view of all students. Every student should be able to easily see you at all times. Your arrangement should continue to utilize social distancing criteria because the closer students are to each other the greater the chance for off-task behaviors.

Years ago, I developed what was called the TREAT Program (Teachers Recognizing Educationally Appropriate Traits) as a principal of an elementary school. It was simple to use and very effective in helping to encourage positive student behaviors. All the elementary school employees (especially teachers) carried small TREAT tickets with them that were given to students when they did something especially positive. This could be exemplary behavior on the playground, and in the classroom or something as simple as opening a door for an adult or being helpful to another student. Emphasis was given to classroom behavior and performance. We were careful not to saturate the program by giving too many positive tickets. When given a ticket the student simply wrote their full name on the ticket and deposited the ticket in bins placed throughout the school. All the employees carried the tickets and could give them to students when appropriate. A TREAT ticket may be given to a student who, without directions, cleaned a lunch table or helped their teacher clean the classroom after school.

At the end of each quarter of school, an assembly was scheduled to draw names from the TREAT bin for special prizes furnished by teachers, businesses, or the parent-teacher group. Students understood the better they behaved, and the more TREAT tickets they received, the better the chance their name would be drawn for a special prize. The TREAT program was so successful that businesses routinely supported the program by donating dozens of bicycles, music CDs, small stereos, stuffed animals, and new book bags, to name a few. The program was a very successful school positive discipline program.

Elementary School Recommendation 3:

Develop regular student assessment programs and share academic progress with parents. Interacting with both students and parents is very important. Review student progress with parents and students regularly. Make sure the students and parents understand your assessment program. Communicate your academic expectations with parents and students early in the school year. Send a positive letter to your new students describing your student management program and expectations for students prior to the first day of school. Include your school's student handbook if available.

Elementary School Recommendation 4:

Seek out programs or teachers who consistently produce higher student performance as noted in formal testing programs. Find out what they are doing to be successful. This is especially important for new teachers who want to improve overall student performance. Concentrate on the tested skills as they are likely the most basic and important skills. The ability to carefully coordinate your instruction to formal assessment will reap significant rewards in student performance.

Elementary School Recommendation 5:

Review effective school research, especially if not emphasized in your teacher-training program. Use your computer to search for what works best. Effective school research will help you create the best instruction for your students.

Elementary School Recommendation 6:

Plan your instruction every day as if you are going to be visited or evaluated by your principal. Concentrate on the skills that are tested in assessment programs. Make sure your students understand what skills are to be addressed and work to make sure the students master those skills with both formal and informal assessment methods.

Chapter 28

SCHOOL BOARD RECOMMENDATIONS

*I **have been*** fortunate to work with many great school boards, several of which won acclaim from the State School Boards Association. Consequently, I have some general recommendations that may help you become even more effective as a school board member.

1. You represent the constituents of your district. Make sure you allow them to express their opinion either in a work session or in the call to the public section of your board meeting. You have the right to demand appropriate decorum during the meeting but allowing people to express their opinions is an important part of your job.

2. Make sure you are making all decisions based on their effect on the students you serve!

3. Understand the difference between a goal and an objective. Goals are more general in nature with objectives being specific strategies used to meet general goals. At least once a year, insist that the

board set several measurable goals and review specific progress throughout the school year. As an example, one school board goal may be to improve student performance. Then ask your administrators to develop measurable objectives to meet that goal. One objective may include enhancing primary reading performance by including one-half hour of intensive phonics for all children in K-3. The objectives and the goals should be measurable.

4. Insist the administration provide you with appropriate backup materials for your board meeting agendas and give adequate time to review supporting materials prior to the scheduled meeting. Developing comprehensive board packets can be difficult, especially in smaller or medium-sized districts that have less administrative support. However, good board packet materials will help organize school board meetings. Insist on the inclusion of comprehensive information that will help you make appropriate decisions. Meet with your superintendent before the meeting if you have any questions about agenda items.

5. Your school board meeting agendas should be posted well in advance of the meeting. As superintendent, I chose to not only post the agenda items but also my recommendations for each action item. After clearly stating my recommendation I always included the phrase "Action as deemed necessary by the governing board." This makes sure people

understand that there will be some type of action on agenda items. Posting administrative recommendations provides more information for the staff and parents in the community. This should speed up meetings so the governing board has more time to deal with more controversial or difficult issues. Board meetings should be only about two hours in length, with a few exceptions. The degree of organization for the meeting is likely correlated with its effectiveness.

6. It might be helpful to schedule board meetings once per month with a board work session in between. Do not burden your administrators with excessive paperwork, but make sure they provide you with backup materials that might end up as a board action item.

7. Carefully review all testing information annually and insist that your superintendent or administrator provides you with specific performance about your schools. Make sure your administration understands how important it is to track student performance from year to year. Ask the administration how your schools rank in comparison to the other schools in your state.

8. Give your superintendent or administrator sufficient time to provide all appropriate backup materials for every board meeting, particularly if you

want action or information items included on the agenda.

9. Although you should make yourselves available to the community and teachers, make decisions based on factual information. While you need to listen to teachers, administrators or parents, do not let them keep you from making decisions that may be better for the students. If you disagree with potential action items, take the time to meet with your superintendent to discuss the issue before the meeting.

10. Regularly visit the schools you represent. This may provide you with useful information to assist you in your role as a school board member.

Poor Governing Board Decision-Making

At one time, I was the superintendent of a district that consisted of many white collar parents who, for the most part, supported and cared deeply about the quality of education. The academic performance of the district's students was the best in the area and state. The district consisted of many retirees and parents whose children were older. The district was the only remaining K-12 unified district in the state but served only students in grades K-9 because they did not have a high school facility. As a result, the district had to pay tuition to a neighboring school district for students in grades 10 through 12. The high school they attended was a good school whose reputation for athletics and scholarship was excellent.

Unfortunately, the charges for those students' tuition exceeded the amount of money our district received in state assistance. In short, the neighboring school district was making significantly more money from excessive tuition charges for our students than what they would have received in state aid. Since the excessive tuition charges were much greater than what our district received in state aid, serious funding issues were created for our district. Parents who were supportive of the high school of attendance seemed convinced that a high school was not needed, failing to recognize the fact that the district needed its own high school from both an academic and financial standpoint.

I was convinced that we would be able to deliver an outstanding educational program as we were already the highest performing school district in the area. Many of the parents of students attending the tuition high school were interested in athletics and felt the student-athletes in a smaller school might not get as much attention from colleges in a smaller school. I was unable to convince them that a track athlete that could run a sub 10-second 100-yard race would get attention regardless of the size of their high school.

Given the academic and athletic quality of the district's students, a new high school would ultimately be a "powerhouse" in all respects. Some parents failed to recognize a new high school could be built and deliver a first-class academic program equal to or better than the other high school. Without a high school, the district was forced to use some elementary state aid to support the extracurricular programs for its students in grades 7 through 9.

Even with a new high school for the district, the parents were able to continue to send their children to the non-district high school. Some of the opposition to the new high school wrongly argued that parents choosing the non-district high school would be required to pay their own tuition. All districts can accept non-resident students and receive the same state aid as their resident students. Our district advertised the fact that their students would be able to attend the high school of their choice since the amount of state aid a district receives is based on its student population or what is called average daily membership.

With a new high school, the district would no longer have to pay excessive tuition because the district would also be able to offer a high school program for all students in grades 10 through 12. We could provide a superior academic program and stressed the fact that more of our students would be able to participate in athletic programs. More of our students could participate in extracurricular programs.

I successfully applied for additional funding from the state to build a new high school. The state purchased a school site, perhaps the most beautiful high desert land in the country, and approved enough money to build a new high school for our students. At that time the amount of state money allocated to the district would build a beautiful school. In addition, negotiations were ongoing to acquire an additional 1.5 million dollars for a performing arts center to be donated by a well-known artist who lived in the district. The future was bright and the administration and school board were excited to be able to serve some of their own high school students and not have to pay excessive tuition for its students to attend any non-resident high school. The option would still remain open for any of our district high school students to attend any non-district high school at no cost to our district.

A new high school would not have resulted in any additional tax to district residents!

Despite my efforts, several district patrons did not accept or understand the funding problems of the district and were not supportive of a new high school building project. Worse yet, the administration of the district of attendance was strongly opposed to a new school for our district. They knew they would no longer be able to charge the excessive tuition for our students and became active in trying to keep our district from building its own high school.

Many district constituents did not want any new school in the area because they felt that high school students would cause additional problems in their community. They complained about potential noise and traffic and several other problems that they thought a high school might create. One of the parents who did not want a high school filed an environmental claim that the new site had environmentally protected owls on the property because they "heard" the owls hooting. That claim was not substantiated after the site was carefully examined by a federal agency. Sadly, those residents tried everything to prevent the district from getting its own high school. Apparently, our appeal to those parents fell on "deaf ears," even though the parents of all of the high school students could continue to attend the non-district high school.

The problem was more difficult because a school board election was scheduled at the same time we were dealing with the new high school building project. Three existing board members had decided to retire. I didn't blame them considering the level of controversy regarding the new high school issue.

The community elected a new school board that was opposed to a new high school, even though it would not cost district residents any additional tax. They ran a successful campaign to get the older retirees opposed to any new school and elect new board members who they knew would vote to stop the high school building project as well. They were successful in their campaign and also made it known that they would replace any district administrator who supported a new high school. All of the district administrators either retired or took other positions. I also decided it was time to retire and left the district when the new school board eliminated the high school building project. This was the most devastating and inappropriate decision I had ever seen by a school board in my career!

Here is a summary of the problem. The new board members did not focus on the students or the district in making the decision to eliminate the building project. They had their own agenda that did not support the students of the district. They did not apparently care about how their decisions would affect the students and made their decision based on inaccurate perceptions of how a new high school might affect them personally. In addition, they refused to consider the positive impact of a new high school on the district and its students.

Throughout the next few years, it became obvious that the decision to eliminate the construction program was bad for the district and its students. Two of the opposing board members eventually left the school board and the effort to get a new high school was renewed.

Your decisions should always be based on the students you serve. Do not allow yourself to be influenced by hearsay or potentially inaccurate information.

CONCLUSION

As predicted, American students continue to struggle in reading and mathematics instruction. The latest international exam in math literacy is an indication of continued poor performance. U.S. students ranked poorly among the 29 countries participating in the latest testing program.[79] Worst yet, according to the National Center for Education Statistics, both math and reading scores plummeted during the first two years of the pandemic in all areas of the nation. The declines were most significant among the most vulnerable children and widened the racial achievement gap.[80] "These are some of the largest declines we have observed in a single assessment cycle in 50 years according to Daniel McGrath of the National Assessment of Educational Progress."[81]

Parents now have the tools to take control of the factors that affect the quality of education their children receive. All parents have a responsibility to take a more active role in helping improve public elementary education. While some schools have excellent programs, far too many elementary schools are not providing an adequate foundation of skills in the early education years.

Seek quality schools for your children. Demand your schools demonstrate instructional effectiveness and your children do their best in school. Get involved in your children's schools by being active in parent groups or even school board elections. Examine the quality of your school by looking at the performance and insist your school demonstrates improvement in student achievement. Regular checks on your children's academic performance is important so meet with teachers regularly.

Thank you for reading *American Elementary Education: The Longest Pandemic!*

APPENDIX

Parent Contract – "Agreement of Support for the
Fundamental Program"

This is to reconfirm our agreement to participate in the
Fundamental Program. Parent participation will be conducive to the success of this program. The undersigned
parent(s) or guardians(s) of <u>STUDENT NAME</u> agree to
support the total Fundamental School program, an alternative offered by the district.

We will read the student handbook thoroughly and
discuss the various rules, goals, philosophy and procedures for the school and make a sincere effort to be
available for:

1. Facilitating homework efforts by providing a time,
   place, and quiet environment for our children. We
   agree to sign all homework forms indicating that
   we have seen the assignments.
2. Conferences whenever scheduled.
3. Consultation with the teacher, principal or other
   school personnel involved with my child.
4. Participating in parent meetings or school projects.

We agree that we will, upon request of the principal, remove our child from this program if the rules and policies of the school are consistently broken. We also understand that if we find the program is not what we want for our child, we may remove him/her for placement in their regular attendance area school within the district.

PARENT SIGNATURE

ENDNOTES

1   Marva Collins and Civia Tamarkin. Marva Collins Way (Los Angeles: J.P. Tarcher, Inc. 1982).

2   Collins and Tamarkin, Marva Collins Way.

3   National Commission for Excellence in Education. "A Nation of Risk: The Imperative for Educational Reform," 1983.

4   No Child Left Behind Act: An Amendment to the Elementary and Secondary Act of 1965. Washington, D.C., 2002.

5   "Map: A-F Grades, Rankings for States on School Quality," Education Week, September 2021.

6   "The Program for International Student Assessment (PISA) Results from PISA 2018," The Organization for Economic Co-Operation and Development, accessed June 6, 2022, https:// oecd.com.

7   "National Assessment of Educational Progress," National Center for Education Statistics, U.S. Department of Education, accessed June 8, 2019, https://nces.ed.gov.

8   "International Association for the Evaluation of Educational Achievement," Trends in International Mathematics and Science Study (TIMMS), accessed June 7, 2022, https://nces.ed.gov.

9   National Center for Education Statistics, "National Assessment of Educational Process."

10   "The Progress in International Reading Literacy Study," Wikipedia, 2016, accessed June 14, 2022, https://en.wikipedia.org.

11   Trends in International Mathematics and Science Study, "International Assessment of Educational Progress."

12   "American Students Fall in International Academic Tests, Chinese Lead the Pack," U.S. News and World Report, Washington D.C., 2013.

13   The American Heritage Dictionary (Houghton Mifflin Company, 1985).

14   Rudolph Flesch, Why Johnny Can't Read (New York: Harper and Row, 1955).

15   Flesch, Why Johnny Still Can't Read. (New York: Harper and Row, 1983).

16   Ibid.

17   The National Commission on Excellence in Education, A Nation at Risk: The Imperative for Educational Reform (Washington, D.C., 1983).

18   Ibid.

19   Patrick Dallabetta, "Maximizing Learning Time: Practical Strategies from Experience and Research," (A presentation to the National Academy of School Executives, Silver Creek, Colorado, July 24, 1984).

20   David Berliner, "The Beginning Teacher Evaluation Study: An Overview and Selected Findings, 1975-1976," Far West Lab for Educational Research and Development, Berkeley, California, 1975.

21 Berliner, "The Beginning Teacher Evaluation Study."

22 Collins and Tamarkin, Marva Collins Way.

23 President's Council on Fitness, Sports, and Nutrition, "President's Challenge," 1966.

24 Patrick Dallabetta, "The Standardized Testing of First Grade Students in Nogales, Arizona by Language Dominance" (Doctoral dissertation, Northern Arizona University, 1980).

25 Evertson, Emmer, Sanford, Clements, "Improving Classroom Management: An Experiment in Elementary School Classrooms," (A Presentation to the American Educational Research Association, New York, 1982).

26 David Aspy and Flora Roebuck, "An Investigation of the Relationship Between Student Levels of Cognitive Functioning and the Teacher's Classroom Behavior," The Journal of Educational Research, Taylor & Francis Group, Oahu, Hawaii, 1972.

27 Arizona Department of Education, accessed February12, 2021, https://azed.edu.

28 STEMSchools, accessed June 4, 2021, https://stem-school.com.

29 "AZ School Report Cards," Arizona Department of Education, accessed October 26, 2020, https://azreportcards.azed.gov.

30 Arizona Department of Education, accessed February 12, 2021, https://azed.edu.

31 Ibid.

32 Arizona Department of Education, accessed February 15, 2021, https://azed.edu.

33 "Arizona School Rankings," SchoolDigger, accessed January 22, 2022, https://schooldigger.com.

34 NICHE, "School Rating Information," accessed May 2, 2022, https://niche.com.

35 Hilda Mosse, The Complete Handbook of Children's Reading Disorders (New York: Human Sciences Press, Inc., 1982).

36 "Annual Survey of School System Finances," U.S. Census Bureau, 2016.

37 National Alliance for Public Charter Schools, 2016, accessed June 2, 2022, https://publiccharters.com.

38 Suzanne Hiscox, How to Increase Learning Time: A Tool For Teachers (Northwest Regional Educational Laboratory, June 6, 1982).

39 Arizona Department of Education, accessed June 2022, https://azed.edu.

40 Ibid.

41 National Center for Education Statistics, "National Assessment of Educational Process."

42 Arizona Department of Education, accessed June 2022, https://azed.edu.

43 Ibid.

44 BASIS Schools, accessed February 2022, https://basised.com.

45   American Federation of Teachers, accessed December 10, 2022, https://aft.org.

46   "The Shame of the Teacher's Unions," The National Review, accessed June 9, 2020, https://nationalreview.com.

47   Wallace Foundation, 2022, accessed June 13, 2022, https://wallacefoundation.org.

48   "We Need to Teach the Truth About Systemic Racism, Say Educators," National Education Association, 2022, accessed June 9, 2022, https://nea.org.

49   "The 1619 Project," New York Times, 2022, accessed June 11, 2022, htpps://nytimes.com.

50   Patrick Groff, Preventing Reading Failure: An Examination of Myths of Reading Instruction (Portland: National Book Company, 1987).

51   Romalda and Walter Spalding, The Writing Road to Reading, (New York: Morrow Company, 1957).

52   Spalding Foundation, 2022, accessed June 6, 2022, htpps://spalding foundation.org.

53   Ibid.

54   R.C. Anderson, E.H. Heibert, J.A. and Scott, I Wilkinson, Becoming a Nation of Readers: The Report of the Commission on Reading (Washington, D.C.: U.S. Department of Education National Academy of Education, 1985).

55   William J. Bennett, First Lessons: A Report on Elementary Education in America (Washington, D.C.: Elementary Education Study Group, 1986).

56   Gary Bitter and Mary White, "Evaluation Study of the Writing Road to Reading," (Arizona State University, 2009).

57   University of Oregon. "Dynamic Indicators of Basic Early Intervention (DIBELS 8th Edition)," (Eugene: University of Oregon College of Education Center on Teaching and Learning, 2018).

58   Snow, Burns, and Griffin, Preventing Reading Difficulties in Young Children, (Washington, D.C., National Reading Panel, 1998).

59   Edward Zeigler, "Why Our Children Aren't Reading," Reader's Digest, reprint from The New York Times, 1985.

60   Brandt Pryor, "Streams of Knowledge, Streams of Action: The River of Research and Development at Technology Based Learning and Research," Arizona State University, 1992.

61   Arizona Department of Education, accessed March 4, 2021, https://azed.edu.

62   Arizona Department of Education, accessed March 8, 2021, https://azed.edu.

63   Spalding Foundation, accessed June 23, 2021, https://spaldingeducation.org.

64   Arizona Department of Education, accessed March 25, 2021, https://azed.edu.

65   Bruno Bettelheim, The Use of Enchantment: The Meaning of Importance of Fairy Tales, (New York, New York: Alfred Knoft Co., 1976).

66 Romalda and Walter Spalding, Writing Road to Reading.

67 Rudolph Flesch, Why Johnny Can't Read.

68 Romalda and Walter Spalding, Writing Road to Reading.

69 Mosse, The Complete Handbook of Children's Reading Disorders.

70 Ibid.

71 Snow, Burns, and Griffin, Preventing Reading Difficulties in Young Children.

72 Arizona Department of Education, accessed March 4, 2021, https://azed.edu.

73 NICHE, accessed May 6, 2021, https://niche.com.

74 Zillow, accessed July 5, 2022, https://zillow.com.

75 Arizona Department of Education, accessed March 4, 2021, https://azed.edu.

76 The Center for Public Education (National School Boards Association), "Key Lessons: What Research Says About the Value of Homework", accessed June 11, 2022, https://nsba.org.

77 Mosse, The Complete Handbook of Children's Reading Disorders.

78 Linea Ehri, Simone Nunes, Steven Stahl, and Dale Willows, Systematic Phonics Instruction Helps Students Learn to Read: Evidence from the Readings Meta-Analysis (Washington D.C.: American Educational Review Association, 2001).

[79]   NICHE, accessed May 6, 2021, https://niche.com.

[80]   "National Assessment of Educational Progress,"
       National Center for Education Statistics, U.S.
       Department of Education, accessed October 31, 2022,
       https://nces.ed.gov.

[81]   National Center for Education Statistics, "National
       Assessment of Educational Process."

CPSIA information can be obtained
at www.ICGtesting.com
Printed in the USA
BVHW031042250123
PP14574600001B/2